The Story of the Hawaiian Volcano Observatory—
A Remarkable First 100 Years of Tracking Eruptions and Earthquakes

By Janet L. Babb, James P. Kauahikaua, and Robert I. Tilling

General Information Product 135

U.S. Department of the Interior
U.S. Geological Survey

U.S. Department of the Interior
KEN SALAZAR, Secretary

U.S. Geological Survey
Marcia K. McNutt, Director

U.S. Geological Survey, Reston, Virginia: 2011

For product and ordering information:
World Wide Web: http://www.usgs.gov/pubprod
Telephone: 1-888-ASK-USGS

For more information on the USGS—the Federal source for science about the Earth,
its natural and living resources, natural hazards, and the environment:
World Wide Web: http://www.usgs.gov, Telephone: 1-888-ASK-USGS

Suggested citation:
Babb, J.L., Kauahikaua, J.P., and Tilling, R.I., 2011, The story of the Hawaiian Volcano Observatory—A remarkable first 100 years of tracking eruptions and earthquakes: U.S. Geological Survey General Information Product 135, 60 p., available at http://pubs.usgs.gov/gip/135/.

Library of Congress Cataloging-in-Publication Data
(http://catalog.loc.gov/)

Contents

As molten lava entered the ocean on Kīlauea's south flank in June 2008, seawater flashed to steam, producing a spectacular display of explosively ejected incandescent lava fragments (USGS photograph by David Dow).

Celebrating 100 Years of Service

A Message from the Secretary of the Interior

This year we celebrate the 100th anniversary of the U.S. Geological Survey's Hawaiian Volcano Observatory (HVO), the first such observatory in the United States. Founded in 1912 and initially funded by the Massachusetts Institute of Technology and a group of Honolulu merchants, HVO has been a Federal Government facility since 1919. After being managed by the U.S. Weather Bureau until 1924, HVO has since been administered by agencies in the U.S. Department of the Interior, including the National Park Service from 1935 to 1947 and the U.S. Geological Survey (USGS) from 1924 to 1935 and again from 1947 to present.

HVO, now located on the rim of Kīlauea Volcano's summit caldera within Hawai'i Volcanoes National Park, monitors the volcanic and seismic activity of Hawaiian volcanoes. These include Kīlauea and Mauna Loa—two of the most active volcanoes in the world. Kīlauea has erupted 48 times in the past 100 years, with a nearly continuous flank eruption since 1983 and an ongoing summit eruption since 2008. Mauna Loa, the largest volcano on Earth, has erupted 13 times under HVO's watch, most recently in 1984, when lava flowed to within 4 miles of Hilo, the largest city on the Island of Hawai'i.

During the past century, HVO has been at the forefront of developing and applying the modern techniques and instruments now used in volcano monitoring, including volcanic-gas monitors, satellite-based deformation measurements, networks of remote cameras recording eruptive activity, and seismic networks such as the Hawai'i Regional Seismic Network. The first seismic network in the USGS was installed on Kīlauea in the 1950s, and earthquake monitoring has been important both as a tool for volcano monitoring and for assessing seismic hazards in the State of Hawaii. HVO has been a training ground for volcanologists from the United States and around the world. Scientists trained at HVO served as the core USGS team that responded to the volcanic unrest and eruption at Mount St. Helens, Washington, in 1980.

Assessing volcanic and seismic hazards is a critical part of HVO's mission. With more than 200 homes on the Island of Hawai'i destroyed by lava flows and damaging earthquakes during the past 30 years, and the ever-present hazards of Hawai'i's active volcanoes, HVO scientists play a key role in ensuring the safety of residents and visitors. By providing crucial and timely volcano and earthquake hazard data, HVO helps Hawai'i County Civil Defense and other public safety agencies mitigate loss of life and property.

When geologist Thomas A. Jaggar founded HVO in 1912, he recognized the need for communicating volcano and earthquake information to the public. Today, HVO scientists carry on the tradition of regularly communicating with the public through weekly articles in local newspapers and on the HVO website, a dynamic website with features such as daily eruption updates, webcam images of current volcanic activity, and maps of recent earthquake activity.

January is "Volcano Awareness Month" on the Island of Hawai'i. In January 2012, HVO will again promote volcano and earthquake awareness through its centennial celebration events and annual series of public talks. These events will begin a year-long celebration of the founding of the Hawaiian Volcano Observatory. We look forward to HVO's next 100 years!

Ken Salazar

Secretary of the Interior

The Hawaiian Volcano Observatory, perched on the rim of Kīlauea Volcano's summit caldera, overlooks Halema‘uma‘u Crater, where a new vent that opened in 2008 continues to emit a volcanic gas plume today (USGS photograph by Michael P. Poland).

The Story of the Hawaiian Volcano Observatory—A Remarkable First 100 Years of Tracking Eruptions and Earthquakes

By Janet L. Babb, James P. Kauahikaua, and Robert I. Tilling

Centennial *Mahalo*

The year 2012 marks the centennial of the Hawaiian Volcano Observatory (HVO). With the support and cooperation of visionaries, financiers, scientists, and other individuals and organizations, HVO has successfully achieved 100 years of continuous monitoring of Hawaiian volcanoes. As we celebrate this milestone anniversary, we express our sincere mahalo—thanks—to the people who have contributed to and participated in HVO's mission during this past century.

First and foremost, we owe a debt of gratitude to the late Thomas A. Jaggar, Jr., the geologist whose vision and efforts led to the founding of HVO. We also acknowledge the pioneering contributions of the late Frank A. Perret, who began the continuous monitoring of Kīlauea in 1911, setting the stage for Jaggar, who took over the work in 1912.

Initial support for HVO was provided by the Massachusetts Institute of Technology (MIT) and the Carnegie Geophysical Laboratory, which financed the initial cache of volcano monitoring instruments and Perret's work in 1911. The Hawaiian Volcano Research Association, a group of Honolulu businessmen organized by Lorrin A. Thurston, also provided essential funding for HVO's daily operations starting in mid-1912 and continuing for several decades.

USGS photograph by Janet L. Babb

Since HVO's beginning, the University of Hawai'i (UH), called the College of Hawaii until 1920, has been an advocate of HVO's scientific studies. We have benefited from collaborations with UH scientists at both the Hilo and Mānoa campuses and look forward to future cooperative efforts to better understand how Hawaiian volcanoes work.

The U.S. Geological Survey (USGS) has operated HVO continuously since 1947. Before then, HVO was under the administration of various Federal agencies—the U.S. Weather Bureau, at the time part of the Department of Agriculture, from 1919 to 1924; the USGS, which first managed HVO from 1924 to 1935; and the National Park Service from 1935 to1947.

For 76 of its first 100 years, HVO has been part of the USGS, the Nation's premier Earth science agency. It currently operates under the direction of the USGS Volcano Science Center, which now supports five volcano observatories covering six U.S. areas—Hawai'i (HVO), Alaska and the Northern Mariana Islands (Alaska Volcano Observatory), Washington and Oregon (Cascades Volcano Observatory), California (California Volcano Observatory), and the Yellowstone region (Yellowstone Volcano Observatory).

Although the National Park Service (NPS) managed HVO for only 12 years, HVO has enjoyed a close working relationship with Hawai'i Volcanoes National Park (named Hawaii National Park until 1961) since the park's founding in 1916. Today, as in past years, the USGS and NPS work together to ensure the safety and education of park visitors. We are grateful to all park employees, particularly Superintendent Cindy Orlando and Chief Ranger Talmadge Magno and their predecessors, for their continuing support of HVO's mission.

HVO also works closely with the Hawai'i County Civil Defense. During volcanic and earthquake crises, we have appreciated the support of civil defense staff, especially that of Harry Kim and Quince Mento, who administered the agency during highly stressful episodes of Kīlauea's ongoing eruption.

Our work in remote areas on Hawai'i's active volcanoes is possible only with the able assistance of Hawai'i County and private pilots who have safely flown HVO staff to eruption sites through the decades. A special mahalo goes to David Okita, who has been HVO's principal helicopter pilot for more than two decades. Many commercial and Civil Air Patrol pilots have also assisted HVO by reporting their observations during various eruptive events.

Hawai'i's news media—print, television, radio, and online sources—do an excellent job of distributing volcano and earthquake information to the public. Their assistance is invaluable to HVO, especially during times of crisis.

HVO's efforts to provide timely and accurate scientific information about Hawaiian volcanoes and earthquakes succeed only because of *you*, our receptive and keenly aware public. By following the activity of Hawai'i's active volcanoes through our daily eruption updates posted on the HVO website, viewing HVO webcam images, reading our weekly "Volcano Watch" articles, and attending our public lectures, you help us to ensure that you can live safely with Hawai'i's dynamic volcanoes.

To everyone who has shared in HVO's reaching this milestone—100 years of continuous volcano monitoring—we extend our deepest gratitude.

Mahalo nui loa!

An HVO geologist explains the latest information on Mauna Loa at a public outreach event in 2009 marking the 25th anniversary of the volcano's most recent eruption. HVO's efforts to provide timely and accurate information about volcanoes and earthquakes succeed only because you, the public, help us to ensure that you can live safely with Hawai'i's dynamic volcanoes. (USGS photograph by Janet L. Babb.)

The History of America's First Volcano Observatory

The Hawaiian Volcano Observatory (HVO), the first volcano observatory in the United States, is located on the west rim of Kīlauea Volcano's summit caldera. For the past 100 years, HVO scientists have monitored Hawai'i's active volcanoes and associated earthquakes. The rich history of the observatory and some of the scientific achievements of HVO's staff during the past century are summarized below.

The Founding of HVO

The history of HVO begins with a geologist named Thomas A. Jaggar, who witnessed the deadly aftermath of volcanic and seismic activity during a decade-long exploration of volcanoes around the world. The devastation he observed, particularly that caused by the 1902 eruption of Mount Pelée on the Caribbean Island of Martinique, led Jaggar to his vision and life-long work to "protect life and property on the basis of sound scientific achievement" by establishing Earth observatories throughout the world.

In 1909, while on his way to study seismic observatories in Japan, Jaggar stopped in Hawai'i, where he visited Kīlauea Volcano for the first time. Noting the volcano's persistent and relatively benign eruptions, accessibility, and frequent earthquakes, Jaggar concluded that Kīlauea was the ideal site for the careful and systematic study of volcanic and seismic activity. He then set about raising funds to build the first American volcano observatory at Kīlauea on the Island of Hawai'i.

Jaggar, a professor at the Massachusetts Institute of Technology (MIT), was unable to immediately relocate to Hawai'i. But by October 1910, with funds from the Edward and Caroline Whitney Estate endowment administered by MIT, he had purchased specialized equipment and had it shipped to Honolulu in anticipation of starting his work on Kīlauea.

In early 1911, Jaggar convinced Frank A. Perret, a world-famous American volcanologist he had met on Vesuvius Volcano in Italy, to travel to Hawai'i to begin the observations of Kīlauea's volcanic activity. From July to October 1911, Perret conducted experiments and documented the lava lake activity within Kīlauea's Halema'uma'u Crater, paving the way for Jaggar to pursue his life's goal of using multiple scientific approaches and all available tools for the observation and measurement of volcanoes and earthquakes.

Several prominent businessmen had pledged significant sums of money in 1909 for the establishment of an observatory at Kīlauea, but Jaggar's delay in getting it started had cooled their enthusiasm. However, when Perret so convincingly demonstrated the value of scientific observation and documentation at Kīlauea, these businessmen, who had formed the Hawaiian Volcano Research Association (HVRA), again pledged funding ($5,000 for 5 years) required to cover the daily operating expenses not covered by MIT funds. Continued HVRA support kept HVO going for several decades.

Thomas A. Jaggar, Jr., in 1916 (USGS/HVO photograph).

How HVO Became the U.S. Geological Survey's First Volcano Observatory

When the Hawaiian Volcano Observatory (HVO) was first established, it was through the support of the Massachusetts Institute of Technology, with additional funding provided in 1912 by the Hawaiian Volcano Research Association, a group of Honolulu businessmen. Since then, the observatory has been managed by several Federal agencies, including the U.S. Weather Bureau (1919–1924), the USGS (1924–1935), and the National Park Service (1935–1947). The USGS became the permanent administrator of HVO in 1947. Because the observatory is located in Hawai'i Volcanoes National Park, people often assume that it is administered by the National Park Service, but HVO is part of the USGS Volcano Hazards Program and is the oldest of five volcano observatories in the United States.

MIT eventually granted Jaggar administrative leave to head the observatory effort. He arrived on Kīlauea and took over the continuous study of Hawai‘i’s active volcanoes on January 17, 1912—the date often noted as the founding of HVO. Another interpretation cites the founding date as July 1, 1912, the day the HVRA began funding HVO's operations. It could also be argued that the day Perret began work, July 2, 1911, is when HVO was established.

Although an “official” founding date is not exact, HVO’s centennial milestone—100 years of continuous volcano monitoring in Hawai‘i—is celebrated in 2012, beginning with an observatory open house in January and continuing with other special events throughout the year.

Building a Volcano Observatory

One of Frank Perret’s first tasks on Kīlauea in 1911 was to oversee the construction of a scientific station on the eastern edge of Halema‘uma‘u Crater, and by late August, it was complete. Perret lived in the small wood-frame building funded by MIT, which he called the “Technology Station,” until mid-September 1911, when he moved to the Volcano House hotel on the north rim of Kīlauea Caldera.

After Jaggar arrived in January 1912, donations from merchants in Hilo, the Island of Hawai‘i's center of commerce, funded a more substantial wood-frame structure that was built on the northeast rim of Kīlauea Caldera, near the present-day Volcano House hotel in Hawai‘i Volcanoes National Park. The main building contained the Director’s office, a workroom, storage space, a darkroom, and visitors’ accommodations. A basement below it housed the Whitney Laboratory of Seismology. The Technology Station, which had fallen into disuse and was vandalized after Perret left Hawai‘i, was moved to the north rim of Halema‘uma‘u Crater later in 1912. Through the years, additional buildings, such as a machine shop, electric plant, and chemistry lab, were added to the HVO facility on the caldera rim.

Interior of HVO's second Technology Station, showing seismograph on right wall (by Thomas Jaggar, USGS/HVO photograph).

HVO's first "Technology Station" (circled) in 1911 (by Frank A. Perret, USGS/HVO photograph).

HVO's first building in 1912 (by Thomas Jaggar, photograph courtesy of Bishop Museum).

Jaggar on porch of HVO's main building in 1916 (USGS/HVO photograph).

Jaggar at work in the main HVO building in 1916 (USGS/HVO photograph).

In 1940, all of HVO's buildings on the rim of Kīlauea Caldera, except for the Whitney vault, were razed to make way for building the present Volcano House hotel. The plan was to move HVO into a new "Volcano Observatory and Naturalist Building" farther from the caldera rim, but until construction was complete, HVO records, machines, furniture, and other gear were stored in various buildings in Hawai'i Volcanoes National Park. HVO staff shared a crowded space with park staff in park headquarters, which at the time was in the building now known as the 'Ōhi'a Wing of Volcano House.

However, as soon as the Volcano Observatory and Naturalist Building was complete, it was commandeered by the U.S. Army to house the Island Military Headquarters under World War II martial law. This delayed providing HVO with its own operating facility until 1942, when the U.S. Army moved its headquarters to Hilo. HVO occupied the second observatory building, now the site of Kīlauea Visitor Center and the current Park Headquarters, from October 1942 to September 1948.

HVO then moved into a building perched above Uwēkahuna Bluff on the west rim of Kīlauea Caldera. Because of its spectacular views of Kīlauea and Mauna Loa, this building had been used by National Park naturalists for talks and visitor services since 1927. After the building was assigned to HVO in 1948, park offices and visitor services were moved to their present location. A second building, called the Geochemistry Wing, was added to HVO in 1961, almost doubling its available office and laboratory space.

HVO's third building in 1951 (USGS photograph by R.E. Wilcox).

In 1985, construction of a larger building began adjacent to those HVO had occupied for many years. By summer 1986, HVO staff had moved into their present home, which includes the old Geochemistry Wing. HVO's original building at this site was then returned to the National Park Service, which converted it to the present-day Thomas A. Jaggar Museum.

On August 26, 2002, HVO's newest building was formally named the "Reginald T. Okamura Building," in honor of the late "Reggie" Okamura, who joined HVO in 1958 and served as its Chief of Operations and unflappable "voice of the volcano" from 1978 to 1992. For much of his HVO career, Reggie managed a USGS Minority Participation in Earth Science Program, which brought ethnic minority students to work at HVO each summer. In 1995, he received the Department of Interior Meritorious Service Award for "outstanding contributions to volcanological studies, advancing the participation of minorities and volunteers in the Earth sciences, and administrative leadership."

HVO circa 1972. The main building (lower left) is now the Jaggar Museum, but the Geochemistry Wing (top) is still used by HVO today. The storage sheds and water tank were removed in 1985 to make way for HVO's current home. (USGS photograph.)

HVOs newest home (left), with its observation tower, was built in 1985–1986. In 2002, the building was named in honor of the late Reginald T. Okamura (photograph circa mid-1970s). The dedication plaque (shown enlarged, above) can be seen on the front left of the building. (USGS photographs; building and plaque photographs taken in 2011 by Andrew Hara.)

The Legacy of HVO Leaders from 1912 to the Present

On his arrival at Kīlauea in 1912, Thomas Jaggar relinquished his MIT academic duties and was appointed the first Director of HVO. From then until he retired in 1940, Jaggar pursued his goal of mitigating the negative impacts of natural hazards on humans through the continuous study of volcanoes and earthquakes, both in Hawai'i and around the world. After leaving HVO, Jaggar continued his research at the University of Hawai'i at Mānoa until his death on January 17, 1953, exactly 41 years after beginning his work on Kīlauea.

Thomas Jaggar is acknowledged as the founder of HVO, but Frank Perret shares in that honor as the scientist who actually began HVO's long history of continuous volcano monitoring in Hawai'i. Perret, a well-known and highly respected volcanologist, launched Jaggar's vision and efforts to better understand volcanoes and earthquakes by observing and recording Kīlauea Volcano's activity from July to October 1911. During his time on Kīlauea, Perret successfully obtained a temperature measurement of molten lava—the first in the world—and documented his experiments and observations in weekly reports published in a Honolulu newspaper, the prototype for subsequent serial publications that continued until mid-1955. As HVO Director pro tem, Perret set the stage for Jaggar's work on Kīlauea.

Since Jaggar's retirement, the ongoing monitoring and research efforts on Hawaiian volcanoes have been guided by 18 scientists who have served as HVO's "Director" or "Scientist-in-Charge." All these leaders have contributed to a better understanding of Hawaiian volcanoes through their individual expertise and unique perspectives. One scientist, however, played a particularly pivotal role in HVO's history—the late Jerry P. Eaton, who came to HVO in 1953 and served as the observatory's leader in 1956–1958 and again in 1960–1961.

HVO Directors	
1912–1940	Thomas A. Jaggar
1940–1951	Ruy Finch
1951–1955	Gordon A. Macdonald
1956–1958	Jerry P. Eaton
HVO Scientists-in-Charge	
1958–1960	Kiguma Jack Murata
1960–1961	Jerry P. Eaton
1961–1962	Donald H. Richter
1962–1963	James G. Moore
1964–1970	Howard A. Powers
1970–1975	Donald W. Peterson
1975–1976	Robert I. Tilling
1976–1978	Gordon P. Eaton
1978–1979	Donald W. Peterson
1979–1984	Robert W. Decker
1984–1991	Thomas L. Wright
1991–1996	David A. Clague
1996–1997	Margaret T. Mangan
1997–2004	Donald A. Swanson
2004–present	James P. Kauahikaua

Left, in 1911, Frank A. Perret (in dark jacket) and an unidentified assistant carry a sample of molten lava collected from the lava lake in Halema'uma'u Crater (photograph by H.R. Schulz, published in American Journal of Science 1913, used with permission).

Right, Thomas Jaggar, circa 1925, at his desk in HVO (USGS photograph).

Jerry P. Eaton in 1954 manually measuring the arrival times of earthquake waveforms on a seismic record (USGS photograph).

James G. Moore in 1963 measuring ground tilt near Kīlauea's summit with a leveling instrument (USGS photograph).

Robert W. Decker answering questions about Mauna Loa's eruption in March 1984 (USGS photograph).

Whereas Jaggar is honored for his vision of systematic monitoring of volcanoes, Jerry Eaton is credited with bringing many aspects of Jaggar's vision to reality. Eaton developed HVO's first true seismic network, designing numerous instruments and supervising their fabrication. This network served as a prototype on which other "modern" networks in California and other regions were based.

Eaton also devised a precise water-based tilt-measuring system that quantitatively tracks the surface deformation caused by movement of magma (molten rock) within a volcano. These tilt studies led to a model of volcanism, described in a series of landmark scientific publications, that remains fundamentally unchanged to this day. Even after he left HVO for a position with the USGS earthquake program, Eaton continued to support HVO's mission with significant contributions to the observatory's volcano monitoring program.

The many accomplishments of HVO's leaders through the years are amply evident in scientific literature. A few of their notable achievements are highlighted here:

James G. Moore, HVO Scientist-in-Charge in 1962–63, initiated studies that revealed new information about the structure of Hawaiian volcanoes, submarine landslides, and the subsidence of the Hawaiian Islands. His marine investigations complemented ongoing terrestrial volcano monitoring efforts, providing a broader tectonic history of Hawaiian volcanoes.

The legacy of the late Robert W. Decker, who served as HVO Scientist-in-Charge during 1979–1984, includes the systematic monitoring of Mauna Loa and a better understanding of volcanic activity indicators, such as ground deformation, that are useful for forecasting eruptions. He also began "Volcano Watch," a series of columns published in local newspapers, as a means of communicating information about Hawaiian volcanoes and HVO's work to the public.

Studies of Kīlauea lavas by Thomas L. Wright, HVO Scientist-in-Charge during 1984–1991, resulted in the first documentation of the mixing of magmas within Hawaiian volcanoes. Wright oversaw the compilation and publication of HVO's early weekly and monthly bulletins and the start of a bibliographic database of papers on Hawaiian volcanic processes. He also oversaw planning and construction of HVO's current home and the conversion of its old building to the National Park Service's Thomas A. Jaggar Museum, both dedicated in 1987, the 75th anniversary of HVO's founding. Wright continues his studies of Kīlauea Volcano as a USGS Scientist Emeritus.

David A. Clague, who served as Scientist-in-Charge from 1991 to 1996, fostered the study of Hawaiian volcanoes in their entirety, from seafloor to summit. During his tenure, HVO adopted the Global Positioning System (GPS) as a key deformation-monitoring tool and upgraded HVO's computer facilities, seismic network, and gas-geochemistry laboratory. He also revived the weekly "Volcano Watch" articles published in local newspapers and posted online. Clague continues to integrate the processes observed at active Hawaiian volcanoes with studies of submarine volcanism through his work as a senior scientist at the Monterey Bay Aquarium Research Institute in California.

Donald A. Swanson, who ushered HVO into the 21st century, initially worked on Kīlauea Volcano as an HVO staff geologist during 1968–1971. His USGS career then took him to other volcanoes, including Mount St. Helens, Washington, during its catastrophic 1980 eruption, which caused the worst volcanic disaster in U.S. history. In 1996, Swanson returned to HVO, where he served as Scientist-in-Charge from 1997 to 2004. During his years as HVO's leader, Swanson oversaw the startup of HVO's own website and initiated the popular daily online updates of Kīlauea's ongoing flank eruption. He instituted the use of Hawaiian language diacritical marks in all HVO publications, interpreted traditional Hawaiian Pele-Hiʻiaka chants in terms of the geologic origin of Kīlauea Caldera (a large volcanic depression formed by the collapse of an underlying magma chamber), and spearheaded an ongoing study of Kīlauea's infrequent large explosive eruptions. Today, Swanson continues his extensive study of Kīlauea's dynamic behavior as an HVO research scientist.

Left, Thomas L. Wright in 1985 making gravity measurement on Kilauea (USGS photograph).

Center, David A. Clague, circa 1993 (USGS photograph).

Right, Donald A. Swanson in 1995 (photograph courtesy of Richard S. Fiske, Smithsonian Institution).

HVO Staff and Volunteers—The "Heart" of the Observatory

HVO's leaders have successfully guided the observatory's mission, but 100 years of continuous volcano monitoring would not have been possible without the hundreds of dedicated staff (permanent and temporary), associates, student interns, and volunteers who have tirelessly worked to improve our understanding of Hawaiian volcanoes over the past century. HVO's staff has grown from one geologist (Thomas Jaggar) in 1912 to a team of as many as 27 scientists and support staff in 2012. This team consists of experts in geology, seismology, geophysics (deformation), gas geochemistry, electronics, and computer technology, as well as Web design, library and photo archives, management, administration, and public information, all of whom work together to achieve HVO's mission.

HVO's Mission

- **Monitor** active and potentially active Hawaiian volcanoes and associated seismicity,
- **Assess** volcanic and earthquake hazards,
- **Respond** to volcanic crises,
- **Conduct** research on volcanoes and earthquakes, and
- **Inform** responsible emergency managers and affected populace about potential volcanic hazards.

HVO staff and volunteers, September 2011 (USGS photograph by Andrew Hara).

Kīlauea and the Hawaiian Volcano Observatory—Then and Now

Site of the First HVO Building

HVO's first building (circled and enlarged) was located on the northeast rim of Kīlauea Caldera. This site was among the early National Park Service buildings and the former Volcano House hotel (the long building on the other side of the road). (Aerial photograph taken in 1923 by the 11th Photo Section, U.S. Army Air Service, Hawaiian Division.)

Today's Volcano House hotel occupies the site of HVO's first building. The Whitney Laboratory of Seismology, a vault housed beneath the original HVO building, is the raised grassy area (circled) in front the Volcano House hotel. (USGS aerial photograph by James P. Kauahikaua.)

Halemaʻumaʻu Crater from the West Rim of Kīlauea Caldera

This photograph, one of the earliest prints of Halemaʻumaʻu Crater within Kīlauea's summit caldera, was only recently discovered in the HVO archives. It was probably taken by William Tufts Brigham in 1865.

On March 25, 1921, Halemaʻumaʻu Crater, then about 1,200 feet in diameter, was nearly filled to the brim with lava. Note the "islands" that appear to be floating in the lava lake. (USGS/HVO photograph by Thomas A. Jaggar.)

In May 1924, three weeks after the lava lake drained from Halemaʻumaʻu, scores of explosive eruptions blasted mud, ash, and hot rocks from the crater. Rocks ejected during this May 18 event killed a photographer who ventured too close to the crater. At the end of the 18-day-long eruption, Halemaʻumaʻu Crater was twice as wide (about 3,250 feet) and three times as deep (more than 1,350 feet). (Photograph by Kenichi Maehara.)

This 2011 photograph is meant to match the viewpoint of Brigham's 1865 photograph of Halemaʻumaʻu Crater. Note the gas plume from Kīlauea's ongoing summit eruption that began in March 2008. The active vent in Halemaʻumaʻu Crater is now 3,300 feet in diameter and contains an active lava lake. (USGS photograph by Andrew Hara.)

Kīlauea Iki Crater During the 1959 Eruption

Lava flows streaming to the floor of Kīlauea Iki Crater on November 15, 1959, just one day after the eruption began (USGS photograph by Donald H. Richter).

By December 2, 1959, two weeks after the eruption began, a lake of lava about 400 feet deep had largely filled Kīlauea Iki Crater (USGS photograph by Donald H. Richter).

Kīlauea's Upper East Rift Zone—Before and After the Mauna Ulu Eruption

Looking uprift (westerly) from Makaopuhi Crater (foreground) in 1929, 'Alae, and 'Ālo'i Craters and the Chain of Craters Road along Kīlauea's upper East Rift Zone are visible in the middle ground. As a reference point, the small vegetated hill of Pu'u Huluhulu is marked by an arrow. (Aerial photograph by the 11th Photo Section, U.S. Army Air Service, Hawaiian Division.)

The same view in 2011 shows a notable change in the landscape, which now includes Mauna Ulu (circled), a volcanic lava shield built by eruptions during 1969–1974. Mauna Ulu lava flows completely filled 'Ālo'i and 'Alae Craters—now no longer visible—but did not bury Pu'u Huluhulu (arrow). The northwestern part of Makaopuhi Crater was also partly filled by Mauna Ulu flows. (USGS photograph by Christina Heliker.)

Hawai‘i’s Active Volcanoes

The Hawaiian Islands are at the southeast end of a chain of volcanoes that began to form more than 70 million years ago. Each island is made of one or more volcanoes, which first erupted on the floor of the Pacific Ocean and emerged above sea level only after countless eruptions.

Five of the six Hawaiian volcanoes classified as “active”— volcanoes that have erupted in the past 10,000 years and could erupt again—are monitored by HVO. These include Haleakalā on the Island of Maui and Mauna Kea, Hualālai, Mauna Loa, and Kīlauea on the Island of Hawai‘i. Lō‘ihi, a submarine volcano southeast of the Island of Hawai‘i, is also classified as active and is monitored by land-based seismometers and periodic oceanographic surveys.

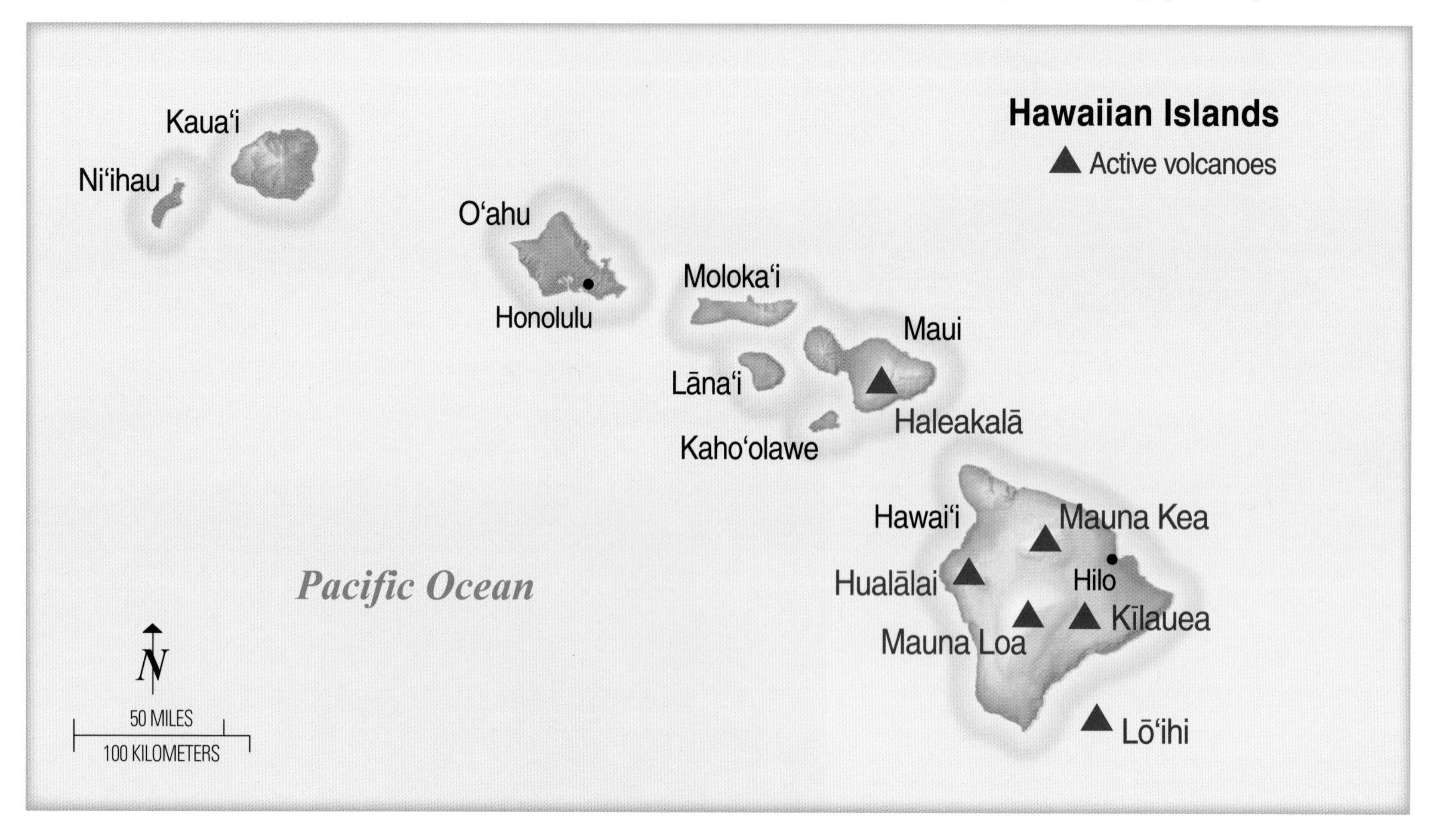

Spectacular sunrise overlooking Mauna Kea and Mauna Loa Volcanoes on the Island of Hawai‘i seen from the top of Hualālai Volcano (USGS photograph by Maurice Sako).

Haleakalā

Recent radiocarbon dating by USGS scientists indicates that Haleakalā on the Island of Maui erupted most recently between about 600 and 400 years ago. HVO uses a sparse network of seismic and other monitoring instruments, as well as onsite field surveys conducted every few years, to track any changes on this volcano, which erupts a few times every thousand years.

Haleakalā summit crater (NPS photograph).

Mauna Kea

Mauna Kea on the Island of Hawai‘i is the highest point in the State of Hawaii at 13,796 feet. The 4,600 years since Mauna Kea’s most recent eruption is a shorter time period than some of its earlier periods of inactivity. Therefore, it is assumed that this volcano’s present inactivity will someday end in an eruption. HVO monitors Mauna Kea, which is not currently showing any signs of volcanic unrest.

Snowcapped Mauna Kea provides a spectacular backdrop for Hilo on the east side of the Island of Hawai‘i in February 2004 (USGS photograph by Donald A. Swanson).

Hualālai

Hualālai is the Island of Hawai'i's third most active volcano. It has erupted three times in the past 1,000 years, with the most recent eruption occurring in 1801. Hualālai has not shown signs of unrest since 1929, when an underground intrusion of magma caused an intense earthquake swarm. However, future eruptions of Hualālai are a certainty, and with expanding urban development on its flanks, diligent volcano monitoring is required.

Hualālai Volcano (USGS photograph by James P. Kauahikaua).

Mauna Loa

Mauna Loa, the largest volcano on Earth, has erupted 33 times since 1843, producing lava flows that have covered extensive areas on its flanks and reached the ocean eight times—along the south, west, and northwest coasts of the Island of Hawai'i. Lava flows less than 4,000 years old cover about 90 percent of the volcano's surface, an indication of Mauna Loa's youthfulness.

When this massive volcano erupts, voluminous and fast-moving 'a'ā flows (rough, blocky lava) can travel from the vent to the ocean in only hours. In 1984, during Mauna Loa's most recent eruption, lava flowed in a matter of days to within about 4 miles of the city limits of Hilo.

Mauna Loa will erupt again and, when it does, it is capable of disrupting lives and commerce throughout the Island of Hawai'i. About two-thirds of the island's residents live in areas potentially affected directly by Mauna Loa's eruptions. Because of this threat, HVO closely monitors this volcano and encourages residents to prepare for Mauna Loa's next eruption.

Mauna Loa, a "textbook" example of a shield volcano, as viewed from the slopes of neighboring Mauna Kea (USGS photograph). Inset, looking from north to south at the summit of Mauna Loa, with a view of North Pit (foreground), Lua Pōholo (small pit crater on left side of North Pit), and Moku'āweoweo, the volcano's main caldera (top center) (USGS photograph by Ben Gaddis).

Kīlauea

Kīlauea, one of the most active volcanoes in the world, is the youngest volcano on the Island of Hawai‘i. More than 90 percent of its surface is covered by lava flows less than 1,100 years old. Kīlauea’s history of numerous and well-known effusive (gently flowing) eruptions has been punctuated by periods of explosive eruptions. The most recent explosive period may have ended in 1790 with an event that killed more than 80 Hawaiians, making Kīlauea the most deadly volcano in what is now the United States.

Kīlauea has erupted essentially continuously since 1983 at Pu‘u ‘Ō‘ō and other vents along the volcano’s East Rift Zone. In 2008, a new vent opened within Halema‘uma‘u Crater at the summit of Kīlauea, which continues to host an active lava lake today.

Lava channel on Kīlauea Volcano’s East Rift Zone in October 2007 (USGS photograph by James P. Kauahikaua).

Volcanic-gas plume emitted from a vent within Halema‘uma‘u Crater at the summit of Kīlauea in November 2008 (USGS photograph by Janet L. Babb).

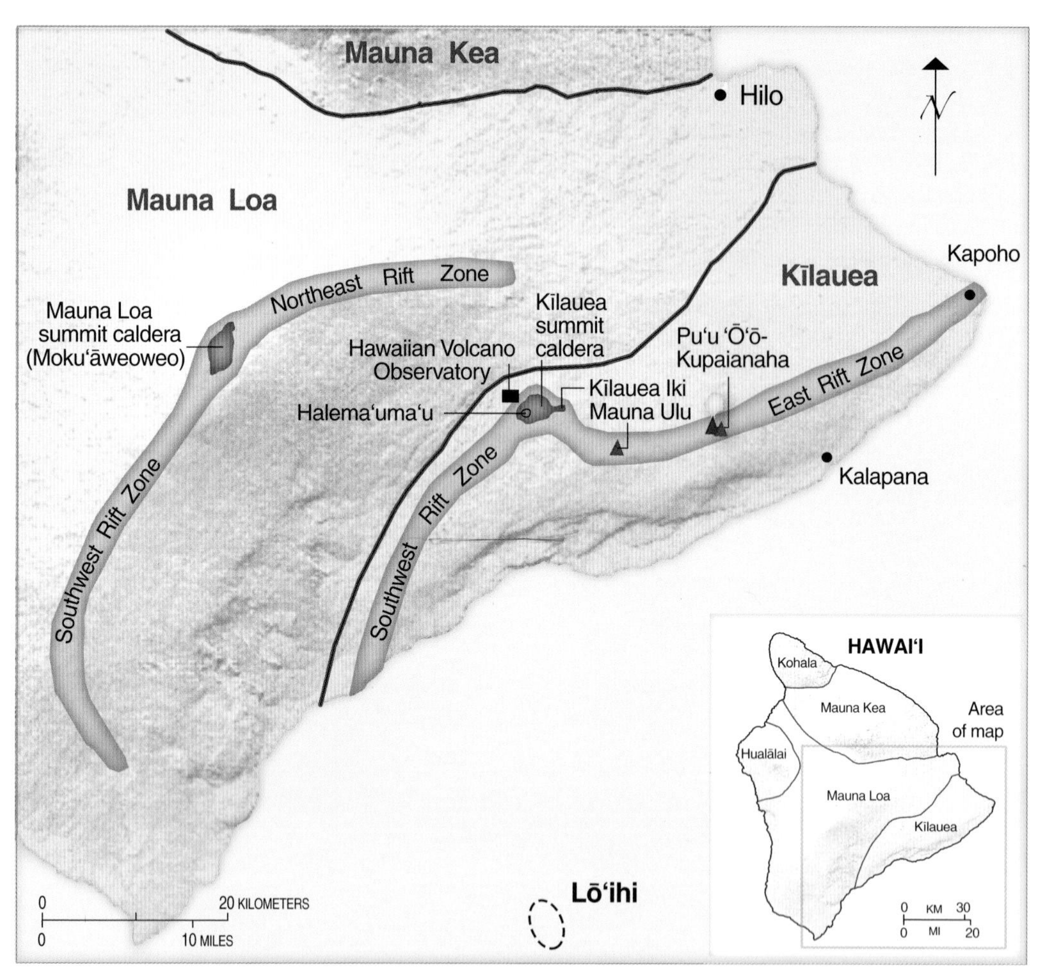

Sketch map showing the summit calderas and rift zones of Kīlauea and Mauna Loa Volcanoes. Also shown are the locations of the Hawaiian Volcano Observatory, sites of some recent eruption vents on Kīlauea, and the growing submarine volcano Lō'ihi offshore to the south. Inset shows all five volcanoes that make up the Island of Hawai'i.

Lō'ihi

Lō'ihi is a submarine volcano about 22 miles southeast of the Island of Hawai'i, and its summit is still some 3,000 feet beneath the surface of the Pacific Ocean. Its submarine topography shows a well-defined summit crater and rift zones. The most recent known eruption of this volcano occurred in 1996. HVO does not monitor Lō'ihi directly, but its eruptions, often accompanied by increased seismicity, can be detected by observatory instruments.

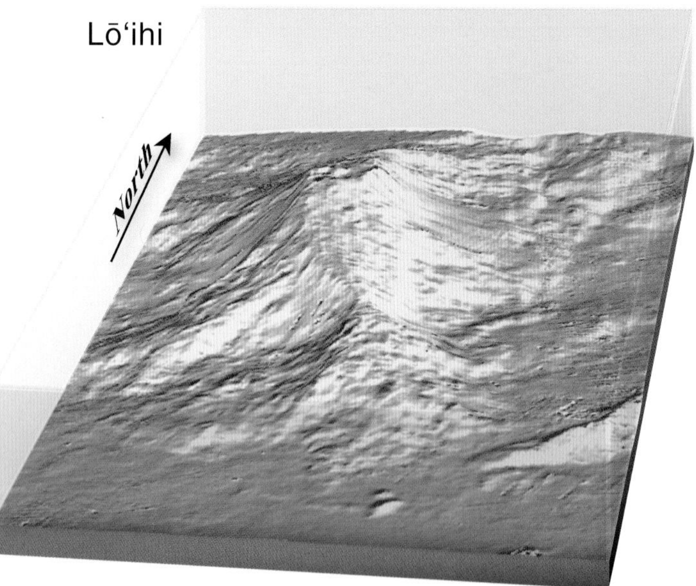

Digital elevation model (DEM) of Lō'ihi submarine volcano, southeast of the Island of Hawai'i. Lō'ihi is the youngest volcano in the Hawaiian Islands chain (USGS image is about 25 miles wide east to west).

A Century of Significant Eruptions and Earthquakes in Hawai‘i

Since Thomas Jaggar founded HVO in 1912, scientists have observed and documented more than 60 volcanic eruptions on Mauna Loa and Kīlauea Volcanoes, as well as numerous strong earthquakes with magnitudes of 6.0 and higher. These events are summarized in the following 100-year-long timeline.

900

1907 Kīlauea summit eruption—From 1907 to 1924, a lava lake within Halema‘uma‘u Crater at the summit of Kīlauea was active almost continuously, except for collapses in December 1916, when lava drained from the crater, and again in 1919, when lava intruded into Kīlauea's Southwest Rift Zone. (USGS/HVO photograph of lava lake in Halema‘uma‘u Crater taken in 1916 by Thomas A. Jaggar.)

1910

1919 Kīlauea Southwest Rift Zone (Mauna Iki) eruption—On December 21, 1919, lava briefly flowed from Kīlauea's Southwest Rift Zone. Two days later, lava erupted from fissures farther down the rift zone and soon formed low shields topped by active lava ponds. The main shield, named Mauna Iki ("Little Mountain"), fed a flow of ‘a‘ā lava (rough, blocky) that reached within 4 miles of the coast by mid-January 1920. In June, as the eruption waned and the lava level subsided, pits formed on the Mauna Iki shield, which remains a prominent landmark on Kīlauea's Southwest Rift Zone. The 221-day-long eruption ended in mid-August 1920. (Hand-colored black-and-white photograph of Mauna Iki lava flow on May 17, 1920, courtesy of Roger and Barbara Myers, photographer unknown.)

1920

1925

1926 Mauna Loa eruption—On April 10, 1926, an eruption began at the summit of Mauna Loa, but fissures soon extended 3 miles down the volcano's Southwest Rift Zone. Three days later, the eruption migrated farther down this rift zone, with three main vents between 7,400 and 8,000 feet elevation, sending massive ʻaʻā flows downslope. The main flow rapidly advanced toward the sea, where it destroyed the small village and harbor at Hoʻōpūloa on the southwest coast of the Island of Hawaiʻi on April 18. The eruption ended on April 26. (Photograph of the destruction of Hoʻōpūloa Village on April 18, 1926, by Tai Sing Loo, courtesy of Hawaii State Archive.)

1924 Kīlauea summit explosions—Kīlauea's first explosive eruption since about 1790 began on May 10, 1924, with a series of explosive bursts in the Halemaʻumaʻu Crater at Kīlauea's summit that increased in violence during the following week. The intensity of the eruption peaked on May 18, when multiple explosions sent black clouds of dust and volcanic ash more than 21,000 feet in to air and blasted a 10-ton boulder about 3,500 feet beyond the crater rim. By the time the eruption ended on May 27, Halemaʻumaʻu Crater was twice as wide (about 3,250 feet) and almost three times as deep (more than 1,350 feet). (USGS photograph of eruption plume 11,500 feet high on May 22, 1924, by Harold T. Stearns.)

1929 Hualālai magnitude 6.5 earthquake—In 1929, more than 6,200 earthquakes rattled the area around Hualālai Volcano from mid-September through November, most likely caused by an intrusion of magma beneath the volcano. Two large earthquakes (each about magnitude 6.5) destroyed houses, water tanks, stone fences, and roadways. Fearing that their homes would collapse, ranch people camped at the ridge of Pu'u Anahulu during the earthquakes in October 1929. The volcanic cone of Pu'uwa'awa'a ("Many-Furrowed Hill") on the northern flank of Hualālai can be seen in the background. (USGS photograph by Thomas A. Jaggar.)

1935

1935 Mauna Loa eruption—On November 21, 1935, an eruption began in Mauna Loa's summit caldera and quickly migrated down its Northeast Rift Zone. On November 27, another vent erupted on the volcano's north flank, well outside the rift zone, sending flows of pāhoehoe lava (smooth, billowy, or ropey) into the saddle area between Mauna Loa and Mauna Kea. Lava flows then turned east toward Hilo, advancing a mile per day, which alarmed residents. In an attempt to divert the flows, then Lieutenant Colonel George S. Patton (later a famed general in World War II) was called on to oversee a U.S. Army operation, suggested by HVO's Thomas Jaggar and Ruy Finch, in which military planes dropped bombs near the eruptive vent on December 27. Jaggar thought the operation was a success, but because the eruption ended just 6 days later, the efficacy of disrupting lava channels with bombs or other explosives remains disputed. (Photograph by 11th Photo Section, U.S. Army Air Services, Hawaiian Division, shows Northeast Rift Zone lava fountains as high as 500 feet on November 22, 1935.)

1940

1942 Mauna Loa eruption—Mauna Loa's "secret" eruption began on April 26, 1942. With World War II underway, nighttime blackouts were imposed on Hawai'i. American officials feared that if the eruption were publicized, the Japanese military could use the bright glow of lava at night to guide warplanes to Hawai'i. The eruption began on the western rim of Mauna Loa's summit caldera but then migrated down the volcano's Northeast Rift Zone. By the time the eruption ended on May 9, lava had reached to within 7 miles of the upper Waiākea Uka area of Hilo. (NPS photograph taken from Kīlauea's summit shows gas plume above Mauna Loa's Northeast Rift Zone on May 2, 1942, by Gunnar O. Fagerlund.)

1950

1950 Mauna Loa eruption—On June 1, 1950, a fissure 1.5 miles long erupted high on Mauna Loa's Southwest Rift Zone, and within 3 hours, 'a'ā lava flows had crossed the main highway on the west coast of the Island of Hawai'i. The flows soon inundated the coastal village of Ho'okena-mauka and reached the ocean, creating billowy clouds of steam that rose 10,000 feet into the air. All the villagers reached safety unharmed, but lava flows destroyed about two dozen structures and cut the highway in three places before the eruption ended on June 23. (Photograph of lava entering the ocean taken in 1950 by Hilo Photo Supply, courtesy of Bishop Museum.)

1951 Kona magnitude 6.9 earthquake—On August 21, 1951, a magnitude 6.9 earthquake struck near Nāpō'opo'o on the west coast of the Island of Hawai'i, generating a small tsunami that was observed in Hilo and Kona. The earthquake was felt as far away as Honolulu, 180 miles from the epicenter, but property damage was most severe in the central Kona district of the Island of Hawai'i, where buildings, water tanks, stone walls, and roads were damaged, some beyond repair. Lower magnitude aftershocks persisted for a month following the main quake. (USGS photograph of a collapsed water tank at Hōnaunau School taken in 1951 by Gordon A. Macdonald.)

1955

1952 Kīlauea summit eruption—Kīlauea Volcano's longest period of quiet in recorded history—almost 18 years—ended on June 27, 1952, when lava erupted in Halema'uma'u Crater. Kīlauea had been quiescent since October 1934, causing some people to wonder if the volcano was dead. But the 1952 summit eruption, which lasted 136 days, put those doubts to rest and proved that Kīlauea was still very much alive. (USGS photograph by Gordon A. Macdonald.)

1959 Kīlauea Iki eruption—On November 14, 1959, a fissure erupted on the south wall of Kīlauea Iki, a crater adjacent to the volcano's summit caldera. Multiple vents along the fissure soon merged into a single main vent. Over the next 5 weeks, high lava fountains gushed from the main vent in 17 separate episodes, flooding the crater to form a lava lake about 440 feet deep. Lava fragments falling from the high fountains formed a cinder-and-spatter cone named Pu'u Pua'i ("Gushing Hill"). Three days before the eruption ended on December 20, 1959, lava was blasted to a height of 1,900 feet above the vent—the highest lava fountain ever measured in Hawai'i. (USGS photograph of lava fountains more than 1,000 feet high in Kīlauea Iki Crater on November 18, 1959.)

1960

1960 Kīlauea East Rift Zone (Kapoho) eruption—On January 12, 1960, HVO detected thousands of small earthquakes north of Kapoho, a village near the eastern tip of the Island of Hawai'i. The next day, larger earthquakes were felt by area residents and deep ground cracks opened through the village—clear indicators that magma was migrating down Kīlauea's East Rift Zone. That night, lava fountains erupted north of Kapoho, accompanied by deafening steam blasts and falling volcanic ash. A thick 'a'ā flow reached the ocean on January 15, and during the next week, lava flows began to spread laterally. Despite efforts to divert the flows with earthen barriers, most of Kapoho was destroyed. Lava extrusion largely ended by February 6, but the main vent emitted volcanic gas, pumice, and cinders until February 20, when the eruption ended. (USGS photograph of Kapoho on January 30, 1960, by Donald H. Richter.)

965

1967–1968 Kīlauea summit lava lake—On November 5, 1967, lava fountains 200 to 250 feet high erupted from vents on the floor of Halema‘uma‘u Crater, forming a lava lake. Twenty-two hours later, the fountains abruptly ceased and lava drained back into the vents. Two days later, the eruption resumed in a pattern of activity—eruption followed by partial draining of the lava lake and a period of quiet—that occurred repeatedly over the next 8 months. By the time the eruption ended on July 13, 1968, lava had filled the crater to a depth of as much as 375 feet. Because this eruption could be easily and safely observed from Crater Rim Drive, it attracted many visitors to Hawai‘i Volcanoes National Park. (Photograph of lava lake in Halema‘uma‘u Crater on December 4, 1967, by C. Stoughton.)

1969–1974 Kīlauea East Rift Zone (Mauna Ulu) eruption—The Mauna Ulu eruption on Kīlauea’s East Rift Zone began on May 24, 1969, but continued well into the 1970s. During the first 2.5 years, the fissure eruption was almost continuous and often spectacular. After a 3.5-month pause in activity (October 1971 to February 1972), the eruption resumed and continued to July 1974, with lava flows covering 17.6 square miles and adding about 230 acres of new land to the Island of Hawai‘i. Repeated overflows from the active lava pond at Mauna Ulu (“Growing Mountain”) also built a volcanic shield nearly 400 feet high. Mauna Ulu was Kīlauea’s longest and largest East Rift Zone eruption in recorded history until surpassed by the ongoing Pu‘u ‘Ō‘ō eruption, which began in 1983. (USGS photograph of lava from Mauna Ulu cascading into ‘Ālo‘i Crater on December 30, 1969, by Donald A. Swanson.)

1970

1973 Honomū magnitude 6.2 earthquake—On April 26, 1973, a magnitude 6.2 earthquake offshore of the Island of Hawai'i, about 15 miles northeast of Hilo, injured 11 people and caused property damage estimated at $5.6 million. The main quake was followed by about 300 aftershocks. (Photograph of damage to coastal structures taken by Larry S. Kadooka, Hawaii Tribune-Herald, used with permission.)

1975

1975 Mauna Loa eruption—Following 25 years of slumber, Mauna Loa awoke with a spectacular, but short-lived, eruption just before midnight on July 5, 1975. Lava fountains erupted from fissures extending across the length of Moku'āweoweo, Mauna Loa's summit caldera, and into the upper ends of the volcano's Northeast and Southwest Rift Zones. After only 6 hours, activity in the caldera and on the Southwest Rift Zone ended, but lava fountaining continued along the Northeast Rift Zone until 7:30 p.m. on July 6, when all activity ceased. (USGS photograph of fissure eruption on Mauna Loa's Northeast Rift Zone on July 6, 1975, by Donald W. Peterson.)

1975 Kalapana magnitude 7.2 earthquake—Early on the morning of November 29, 1975, residents of the Island of Hawai'i were jarred awake by a magnitude 7.2 earthquake—the largest event since the devastating 1868 earthquake, which had an estimated magnitude of 7.9. This 1975 earthquake, located west of Kalapana on the island's southeast coast, caused more than $4 million in damage, including extensive ground cracking and heavy road damage in Hawai'i Volcanoes National Park. The earthquake was closely followed by a tsunami that caused the deaths of two backcountry campers on the park's south coast. Lava also briefly erupted at Kīlauea's summit, apparently triggered by the vigorous ground shaking. (USGS photograph of damage to Chain of Craters Road in Hawai'i Volcanoes National Park taken in 1975 by Robin T. Holcomb.)

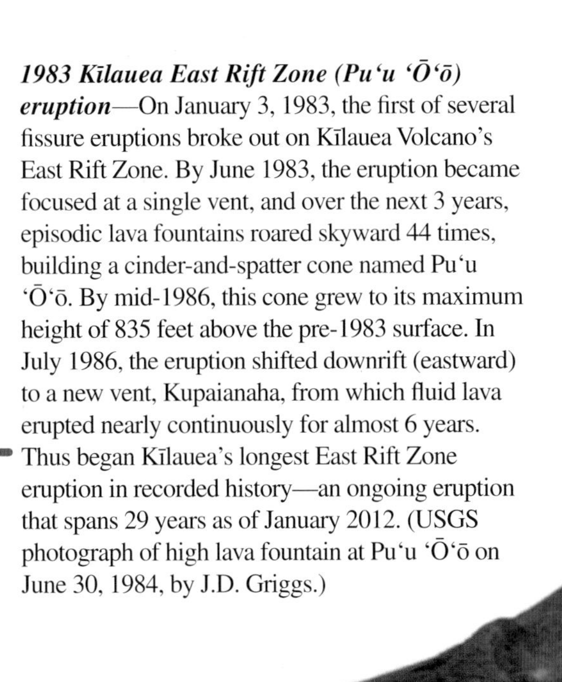

1980

1983 Kīlauea East Rift Zone (Pu‘u ‘Ō‘ō) eruption—On January 3, 1983, the first of several fissure eruptions broke out on Kīlauea Volcano's East Rift Zone. By June 1983, the eruption became focused at a single vent, and over the next 3 years, episodic lava fountains roared skyward 44 times, building a cinder-and-spatter cone named Pu‘u ‘Ō‘ō. By mid-1986, this cone grew to its maximum height of 835 feet above the pre-1983 surface. In July 1986, the eruption shifted downrift (eastward) to a new vent, Kupaianaha, from which fluid lava erupted nearly continuously for almost 6 years. Thus began Kīlauea's longest East Rift Zone eruption in recorded history—an ongoing eruption that spans 29 years as of January 2012. (USGS photograph of high lava fountain at Pu‘u ‘Ō‘ō on June 30, 1984, by J.D. Griggs.)

1983 Ka'ōiki magnitude 6.6 earthquake—On the morning of November 16, 1983, a magnitude 6.6 earthquake struck along the Ka'ōiki fault, a zone of high seismicity beneath the southeast flank of Mauna Loa. Intense shaking caused sections of Hawai'i Volcanoes National Park's Crater Rim Drive to fall into the caldera, and extensive structural damage also occurred in Hilo. Total damage was estimated at $7 million, but there were only a few minor injuries. HVO seismographs recorded more than 10,000 aftershocks by the end of the month. (USGS photograph of damage in HVO's library on November 16, 1983, by J.D. Griggs.)

1980

1984 Mauna Loa eruption—Following 18 months of increased seismicity and summit inflation, Mauna Loa's most recent eruption began on March 25, 1984, at 1:30 a.m., when a fissure opened in Moku'āweoweo, the volcano's summit caldera (elevation 13,680 feet). By 4:00 a.m., the eruption had migrated into Mauna Loa's upper Northeast Rift Zone, where active fissures eventually extended downrift to an elevation of 9,300 feet. Fast-moving 'a'ā flows advanced downslope, and in a matter of days, lava was within about 4 miles of Hilo. Fortunately, the eruption ended on April 15 before lava flows could reach the city limits. Since 1984, Mauna Loa has not erupted—its longest quiet period in recorded history. (USGS photograph of two HVO scientists (circled) approaching the main vents on Mauna Loa's Northeast Rift Zone on March 26, 1984, by J.D. Griggs.)

1985

1989 Kalapana magnitude 6.1 earthquake—A magnitude 6.1 earthquake struck the southeast coast of the Island of Hawai'i on June 25, 1989. The earthquake was the result of the seaward movement of the south flank of Kīlauea Volcano. It was felt on the islands of Hawai'i, Maui, and O'ahu, but damage to residential property was greatest in the Island of Hawai'i's Puna District, where several homes in Kalapana, Royal Gardens, and Kaimū collapsed and many other structures suffered significant damage. Total property damage was estimated at $1 million. Although the earthquake generated a small local tsunami, no wave damage was reported. (USGS photograph of house in Kalapana, damaged in the 1989 earthquake, by J.D. Griggs.)

1990

Ongoing Kīlauea East Rift Zone eruption—Kīlauea's ongoing East Rift Zone eruption, which began in 1983, entered its most destructive period in March 1990, when lava flows erupted from the Kupaianaha vent and advanced toward Kalapana, a cherished area on the southeast coast of the Island of Hawai'i. Within a span of 6 months, the entire community, including 100 homes, was buried beneath 50 to 80 feet of lava. The flows kept moving eastward and into the ocean at Kaimū, a black sand beach highly popular with residents and tourists alike, filling the bay there with lava that extended 1,000 feet beyond the original shoreline. In late 1990, lava flows turned westward, away from Kalapana, and headed back into Hawai'i Volcanoes National Park. In 1992, the focus of the eruption shifted back from Kupaianaha to the Pu'u 'Ō'ō vent. (USGS photograph of lava flow entering Harry K. Brown Park in Kalapana on May 7, 1990, by Dorian Weisel.)

0

Ongoing Kīlauea East Rift Zone eruption—Kīlauea's East Rift Zone eruption, which began in 1983, continued, sending lava flows into Hawai'i Volcanoes National Park until 2007, when the eruption shifted downrift and lava flows once again threatened the Royal Gardens and Kalapana Gardens subdivisions. This decade included the two longest-lasting entries of lava into the ocean during Kīlauea's ongoing eruption. Lava flows continually poured into the ocean for 22 months at both East Lae'apuki (2005–2007) and Waikupanaha (2008–2010), affording excellent opportunities to study the formation and sudden collapse of lava deltas. (USGS photograph of steam plume from the West Highcastle ocean entry on January 3, 2003, by Richard P. Hoblitt.)

2005

2006 Kīholo Bay magnitude 6.7 and Māhukona magnitude 6.0 earthquakes—Two earthquakes struck the Island of Hawai'i's northwest coast on October 15, 2006. The first, at 7:07 a.m., was a magnitude 6.7 earthquake centered in Kīholo Bay at a depth of 24 miles. Seven minutes later, a magnitude 6.0 earthquake occurred offshore of Māhukona at a depth of 12 miles. These earthquakes, identified as separate events rather than as a main quake and aftershock, were caused by the bending of the Earth's crust and upper mantle under the weight of the overlying Hawaiian Islands. They were felt throughout the State of Hawaii, but the greatest damage occurred in the North Kona and Kohala Districts of the Island of Hawai'i. (USGS photographs of damaged Kalāhikiola Congregational Church in Kapa'au, near the north tip of the Island of Hawai'i, taken in 2006 by Jane Takahashi.)

2008 Kīlauea summit eruption—On March 19, 2008, one week after vigorous fuming (gas emissions) began near the base of the east wall of Halema‘uma‘u Crater, an explosive event—the first at Kīlauea's summit since 1924—blasted out hot, rocky debris, forming a vent in the crater wall. Thus began Kīlauea's most recent summit eruption, which continues today with a persistent lava lake deep within the vent and continuous emission of volcanic gases. Collapses within the vent and along its rim enlarged the summit vent from 115 feet in 2008 to more than 475 feet in diameter by the end of 2011. It is now a gaping hole that extends onto the floor of Halema‘uma‘u Crater. (USGS photograph of a dusty-brown plume of gas produced by a vent collapse in Halema‘uma‘u Crater on Feburary 4, 2009, by Janet L. Babb.)

2010

Ongoing Kīlauea East Rift Zone eruption—In 2010, lava flows from the ongoing eruption on Kīlauea's East Rift Zone again turned toward the southeast coast of the Island of Hawai‘i, destroying a Kalapana Gardens residence in July. Soon thereafter, the flows shifted direction and entered the ocean west of the subdivision—but only for a while. In late November, the destruction of a second home was followed by another temporary respite. In early 2011, lava flows encroached on Kalapana Gardens yet again, resulting in the loss of another residence—the 213th structure destroyed by lava since Kīlauea's East Rift Zone eruption began in 1983. As HVO celebrates its 100th anniversary in 2012, vents on Kīlauea's East Rift Zone and at the volcano's summit continue to erupt. The duration of the ongoing concurrent eruptions at vents on Kīlauea's East Rift Zone and at its summit is unprecedented for the volcano in recorded history. (USGS photograph showing the frame of a Kalapana Gardens structure overrun by lava on January 18, 2011, by Michael P. Poland.)

Flowing lava erupted from Kīlauea's East Rift Zone burns trees as it advances through a forest in the Royal Gardens subdivision (USGS photograph by Tim R. Orr, February 28, 2008).

"Volcanoes are an important part of life on the Island of Hawai'i. Those of us who live here deal with the consequences of volcanic activity every day—both good and bad. We enjoy the spectacular beauty and drama of active lava flows but grumble about the poor air quality caused by gases from Kīlauea's ongoing eruptions. We appreciate the volcanic soils in which flowers, coffee, and other agricultural products grow but are saddened by the loss of homes burned by lava flows. Hawaiian volcanoes can create new land, but they can also destroy. So, if we choose to live on the Island of Hawai'i, we must learn to live in harmony with the dynamics of its ever-changing environment."

Jim Kauahikaua
HVO Scientist-in-Charge, 2011

One Hundred Years of Volcano Monitoring—The Evolution of HVO's Tools and Techniques

Before an eruption, magma migrates upward or laterally within a volcano, slowly making its way to the surface. This forceful intrusion of magma triggers small earthquakes and causes the volcano to swell (inflate), both of which are key indicators of an impending eruption.

When Thomas Jaggar arrived at Kīlauea in 1912, he monitored seismic activity and changes in the shape of the volcano with the best tools available to him at the time—a few seismometers, some meteorological equipment, and a surveyor's transit. What he lacked in instrumentation, however, he made up for with ingenuity, keen observations, and detailed documentation of volcanic activity using a camera and notebook.

Today, HVO scientists analyze abundant and diverse data collected from more than 100 field stations, each of which consists of 1 to 5 instruments, including seismic, deformation, volcanic-gas, geologic, and other monitoring tools. These field stations transmit data to the observatory 24 hours a day, 7 days a week, with a single instrument sending as much as 60 terabytes of data each year—much more information than Jaggar might ever have imagined possible.

I ka nānā no a ʻike.

(By observing, one learns.)

ʻŌlelo Noʻeau (Hawaiian Proverb)

Thomas Jaggar on the front porch of HVO's first building making a daily meteorological measurement in 1916 (USGS/HVO photograph).

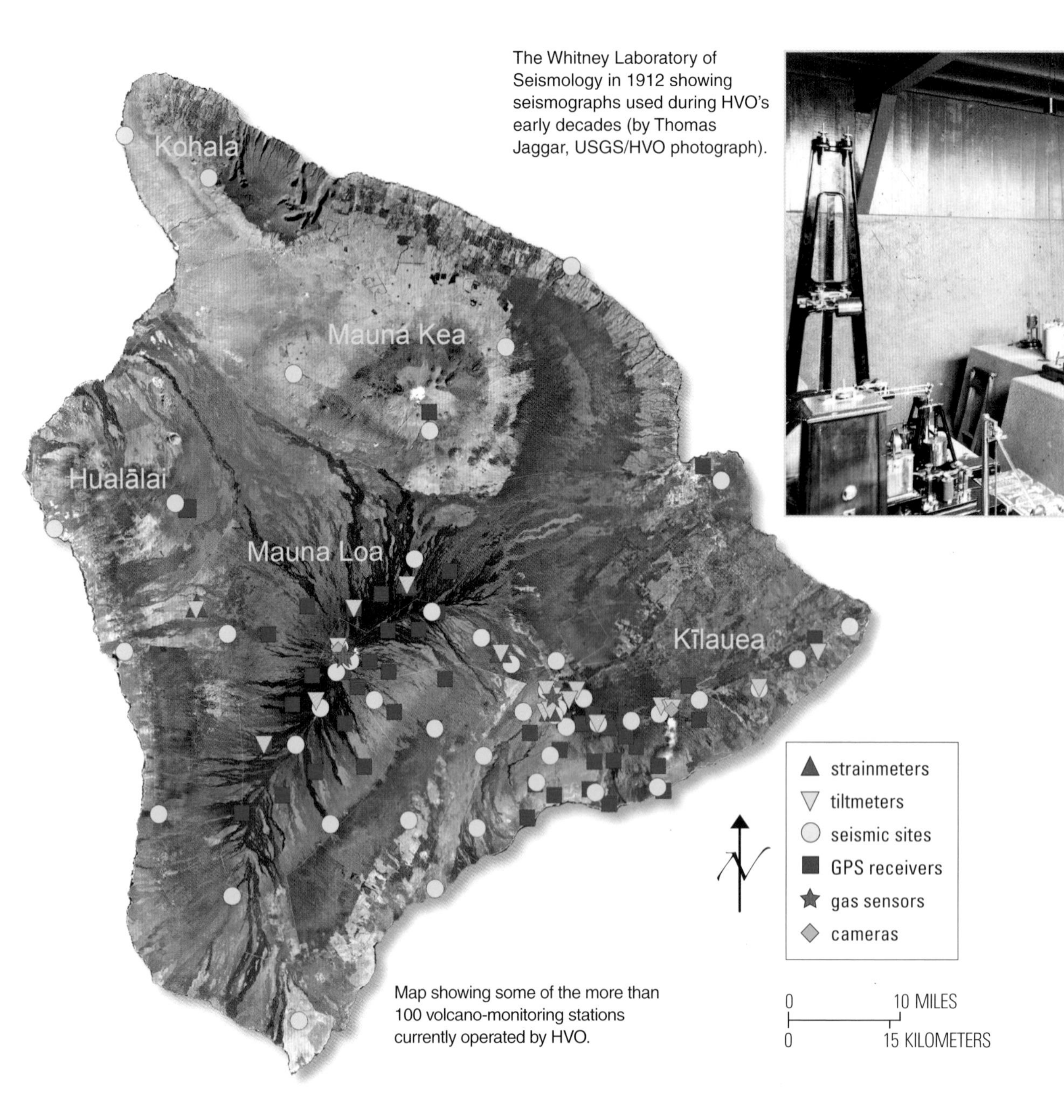

The Whitney Laboratory of Seismology in 1912 showing seismographs used during HVO's early decades (by Thomas Jaggar, USGS/HVO photograph).

Map showing some of the more than 100 volcano-monitoring stations currently operated by HVO.

Seismic Monitoring

Seismicity—rapid ground shaking by earthquakes and tremor—can be caused by the movement of magma within a volcano, so seismic monitoring is one of the main methods scientists use to track volcanic activity. Earthquakes associated with volcanic activity are caused by rock breaking as magma forces its way through underground conduits, whereas volcanic tremor results from the fluid motion of the magma itself. By closely monitoring the number, magnitude, depth, and types of earthquakes, scientists can track the subsurface movement of magma within a volcano and assess whether or not it is rising toward the surface.

Seismic waves produced by breaking rock or magma movement within a volcano are detected by seismometers strategically placed on the surface of the volcano. This information is then converted into digital electronic signals that are transmitted to HVO.

By analyzing signals from multiple seismometers, HVO scientists can determine the time, location, and magnitude of an earthquake.

The first seismometer on the Island of Hawai'i was installed in 1912 in the Whitney Laboratory of Seismology, the basement vault beneath what was then HVO's main building. During the first several decades of monitoring, HVO operated no more than five seismic stations. These early instruments had low sensitivity and imprecise timing mechanisms, so Jaggar could only count the number of earthquakes and estimate their distance from a seismometer. He was also hindered by the fact that it took days or weeks for the paper records from seismic stations beyond the Whitney vault to be delivered to HVO, which meant that he could only compare seismic signals from different stations many days after they were recorded.

HVO's seismic monitoring capabilities were upgraded substantially by seismologist Jerry P. Eaton, who arrived in 1953. He established a true permanent seismic network at Kīlauea, with signals from seismometers transmitted from the field to the observatory through overland cables and, later, wirelessly using ultrahigh-frequency (UHF) radios. These high-quality data allowed scientists to quickly and accurately determine an earthquake's location and magnitude.

Installation of the solar panel and antenna for a seismic station on Kīlauea during HVO's recent upgrade of its seismic network (USGS photograph by Janet L. Babb).

Left, Jerry Eaton, circa 1954, examining earthquake waveforms recorded on "smoked-drum" seismographs (photograph courtesy of Honolulu Star-Bulletin). Below, closeup of a smoked-drum record (USGS photograph by Robert W. Decker).

HVO's seismic network has since greatly expanded, with increases in both the number and sensitivity of seismometers installed on Hawaiian volcanoes. As HVO embraced the computer age, it became possible to record, store, and analyze more seismic data, further improving the scientific understanding of the internal structure of and magmatic pathways within Hawai'i's active volcanoes.

With funding from the American Recovery and Reinvestment Act of 2009, HVO recently upgraded its monitoring network. Today, HVO's seismic network is among the most technologically advanced and densest in the world, with 54 stations digitally recording earthquakes and tremor on Hawai'i's active volcanoes.

Deformation Monitoring

Ground deformation, changes in the shape of a volcano's surface, includes both vertical (uplift or subsidence) and horizontal (extension or contraction) changes, as well as changes in the slope or inclination of the ground surface (tilt). These surface changes are typically quite small by human standards—only fractions of an inch—but they reflect the movements of large amounts of magma within the volcano, so precise measurements are crucial.

Early on, HVO used ground-based instruments and techniques to measure deformation of Hawaiian volcanoes. In recent decades, as remote-sensing technologies became available, HVO began to use satellite-based monitoring tools and methods (so-called "space geodesy").

Repeated leveling surveys were HVO's primary means of measuring vertical deformation on Hawaiian volcanoes until the 1990s. Leveling remains the most sensitive method to measure vertical ground displacements but it has been largely replaced by more modern and versatile techniques.

One end of a water-tube tiltmeter line being used on the summit of Kīlauea Volcano in 1967 (USGS/HVO photograph).

In the 1960s, HVO began tracking changes in horizontal ground distances above magma bodies using electronic distance measurement (EDM), which measures the travel time of a laser fired at a reflector. An increase in the distance between the two fixed points (laser source and reflector) indicates expansion of the magma body (inflation); a decrease in the distance indicates deflation.

EDM was replaced by new technology in the early 1990s, when HVO began using the Global Positioning System (GPS) as a deformation measurement tool. Although the technology applied is basically the same as that for hand-held GPS receivers used by hikers and drivers, the GPS receivers used by HVO have much greater accuracy. HVO now collects continuous data from more than 60 highly sensitive GPS receivers, which track both vertical and horizontal deformation to within a tiny fraction of an inch. In addition to these permanently installed and continuously recording GPS receivers, HVO conducts annual or biannual GPS surveys with portable instruments to supplement the continuous data. Mobile GPS receivers are also used at extremely active sites, such as Kīlauea's erupting flank vents, to measure localized ground deformation.

Ground tilt, another important measure of deformation, was inadvertently recorded on Kīlauea by Jaggar's earliest seismometers, which were built with pendulums that moved during earthquakes. The pendulums also showed long-term deflections that did not yield precise measurements but clearly recorded tilt. Thanks to this unexpected "built-in" monitoring tool, HVO's continuous record of ground tilt at Kīlauea's summit extends back to 1913.

The quality of HVO's tilt measurements improved greatly in the late 1950s, when Jerry Eaton established a network of water-tube tiltmeters.

HVO field crew taking precise measurements of vertical ground deformation at the summit of Kīlauea using a leveling rod (top) and "gun" (left) in 2008 (USGS photographs by David Dow and Kelly Wooten).

HVO scientist in 1968 setting up laser retro-reflector clusters used in electronic distance measurement (EDM) (photograph courtesy of Richard S. Fiske, Smithsonian Institution).

A Global Positioning System (GPS) receiver being adjusted during a 2007 HVO field survey (USGS photograph by Loren Antolik).

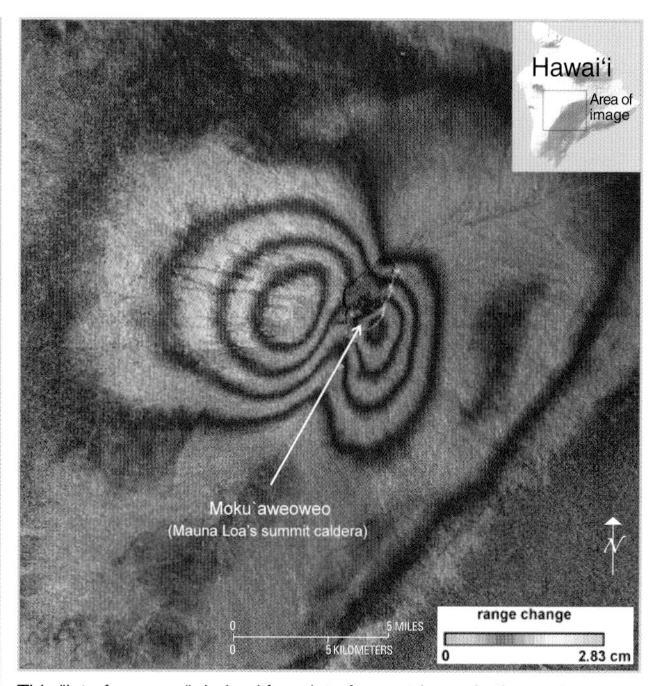

This "interferogram," derived from interferometric synthetic aperture radar (InSAR) satellite data of Mauna Loa's summit area, shows rapid deformation in 2004–2005. The color bands record a complex pattern of several inches of inflation of the volcano's magma reservoir (data courtesy of the European Space Agency).

This technique resulted in precise measurements but was difficult and time consuming.

The first electronic tiltmeter was installed at Kīlauea in 1966, providing HVO scientists with their first truly reliable and continuous real-time monitoring of summit tilt. HVO now has about 20 electronic tiltmeters to monitor ground deformation on Kīlauea and Mauna Loa, Hawaiʻi's two most active volcanoes. These tiltmeters, which are exceedingly sensitive instruments designed to detect tiny changes, excel at recording rapid, short-term events in real time and provide early warning of changes that could lead to an eruption.

Interferometric synthetic aperture radar (InSAR), another satellite-based technology, was first tested at Kīlauea in 1994 and is now routinely used to map surface deformation in Hawaiʻi. With InSAR, radar images of the Earth's surface acquired by orbiting satellites at different times are compared to show subtle ground-surface movements that occur between orbits. The resulting "interferogram" is a detailed map of ground motion directed toward or away from the satellite.

HVO will continue to use a combination of ground- and space-based monitoring networks to help obtain the best picture possible of the inner workings of Hawaiian volcanoes. But based on the technological and scientific progress made in just the past 20 years, the next generation of deformation monitoring tools will likely provide even higher resolution data in unexpected ways, further sharpening our picture.

Volcanic-Gas Monitoring

Early scientific studies of Kīlauea's summit in 1912–1919 included sampling and analyzing volcanic gases, and some of those gas collections are still considered among the best in the world. Following these early investigations, the study of volcanic gases at HVO languished until the 1960s, when there was renewed interest in systematic gas studies during short-lived Hawaiian eruptions. This interest and the development of new technologies for measuring volcanic gases led to the installation of a gas-analysis laboratory at HVO in 1980.

Magma inside a volcano contains a mixture of dissolved gases composed primarily of water (H_2O), carbon dioxide (CO_2), and sulfur dioxide (SO_2). As magma rises to the surface, the pressure on it decreases, which allows the gases to exsolve (bubble out), much like the gas that bubbles out of a soda bottle when the cap is loosened.

HVO scientist collecting a gas sample from a volcanic-gas vent (fumarole) at the summit of Kīlauea (USGS photograph by A. Jeff Sutton).

HVO gas-analysis laboratory in 1983 (USGS photograph by J.D. Griggs).

Measuring the types and amounts of volcanic gases released at a volcano's surface helps HVO scientists estimate the volumes and depths of magma bodies beneath Hawaiian volcanoes. Because SO_2 is not normally present in Earth's atmosphere (unlike H_2O and CO_2), it is one of the easiest volcanic gases to detect. HVO has measured Kīlauea's SO_2 emission rates on a regular and systematic basis since 1979—one of the longest records in the world.

The simplest and oldest way to sample volcanic gas is to collect it directly from a fumarole (a volcanic-gas vent). The sample is sealed in a bottle and then brought to a laboratory for analysis. Although this method has been a mainstay of volcanic-gas sampling for more than a century, field areas where gases are collected can be hazardous to humans and laboratory analyses require time and sophisticated equipment. HVO still uses this method today, but less frequently than in the past.

HVO scientists now use ultraviolet spectrometers to routinely measure the SO_2 emitted from Hawai'i's active volcanoes. These instruments detect the amount of sunlight (ultraviolet energy) absorbed by the SO_2 in a volcanic-gas plume. From 1979 to 2004, HVO used a correlation spectrometer (COSPEC) to measure SO_2 emission rates. Since 2004, a much more compact and less costly ultraviolet spectrometer, called a "Flyspec" for its small size, has been used to measure SO_2. Using data from Flyspec measurements, scientists can calculate the amount of SO_2 in a volcanic-gas plume.

In 2004, HVO geochemists began measuring gases released from Kīlauea with a Fourier transform infrared (FTIR) spectrometer, an instrument that detects gas compositions on the basis of absorbed infrared light. The data obtained from FTIR measurements have been useful in identifying the many components of volcanic-gas emissions, which provide information on the quantity of magma circulating within an eruptive vent.

The newest technology for measuring SO_2 emission rates is ultraviolet spectrometry applied to digital cameras, and HVO scientists are experimenting with how to use this technique on Hawaiian volcanoes. These SO_2 cameras can produce several measurements per minute, more than rapid enough to track most changes in a volcanic system. Comprehensive knowledge of the composition and emission rate of SO_2 and other gases is essential not only to characterize eruptive processes but also to assess the potential health hazards they pose to residents and visitors on the Hawaiian Islands.

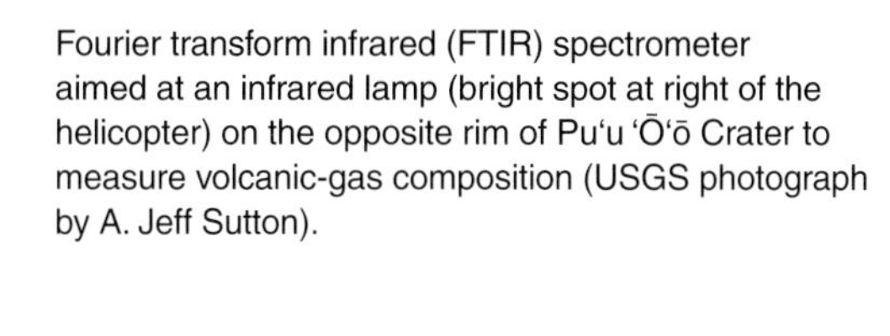

Fourier transform infrared (FTIR) spectrometer aimed at an infrared lamp (bright spot at right of the helicopter) on the opposite rim of Pu‘u ‘Ō‘ō Crater to measure volcanic-gas composition (USGS photograph by A. Jeff Sutton).

An HVO vehicle (circled) drives through the volcanic-gas plume emitted from the vent in Halema‘uma‘u Crater at the summit of Kīlauea. A “Flyspec” compact ultraviolet spectrometer attached to the vehicle’s roof (inset) is used to measure sulfur dioxide gas (SO_2) emissions in the plume. (NPS photograph by Dave Boyle and USGS photograph by Janet L. Babb.)

Geologic Monitoring

Geology lays the groundwork for volcano monitoring, and geologic mapping of volcanic deposits and structures is the initial step to understanding a volcano's past, present, and potential future activity. The first geologic map of the Island of Hawai'i was published in 1946 by USGS scientists Harold T. Stearns and Gordon A. Macdonald. A more recent USGS map of the island, published in 2005, portrays in detail the distribution and ages of lava flows from prehistoric and historical eruptions, confirming, among other things, the youthfulness of Mauna Loa and Kīlauea volcanoes.

Mapping volcanoes has been made easier in recent decades by new technologies, such

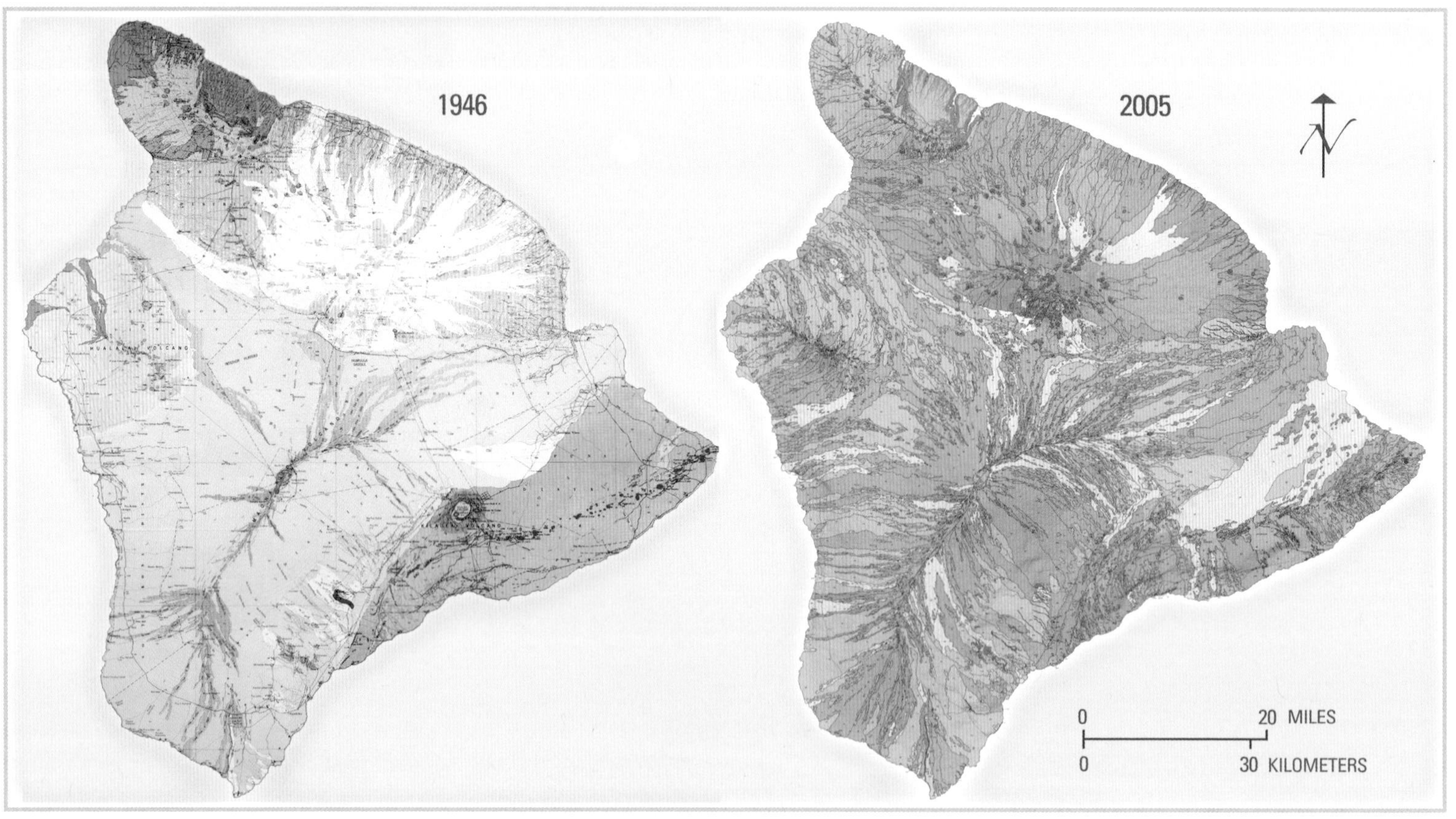

A comparison of USGS geologic maps of the Island of Hawai'i published in 1946 (left) and 2005 (right) shows how HVO's understanding of the island's geology has advanced during the past half century. Both maps use color to differentiate volcanic deposits, but the newer map portrays in greater detail the distribution and ages of lava flows from prehistoric and historical eruptions.

HVO geologists mapping an advancing front of a lava flow on Kīlauea's south flank in 2008 using GPS (left), and mapping a 1,000-year-old lava flow on the heavily forested slopes of Mauna Loa (right) (USGS photographs by Michael P. Poland and Kelly Wooten).

Wearing protective clothing against the intense heat of the lava, an HVO geologist collects a sample of molten lava from a slowly advancing pāhoehoe flow on Kīlauea's south coastal plain (USGS photograph by Janet L. Babb).

as GPS, but still requires a lot of "boots on the ground" work, often in remote and rugged regions. On Kīlauea, which has been erupting continuously since 1983, HVO geologists map active lava flows, sometimes daily, to track the progress of the flows and project their likely future paths—information that is then conveyed to public safety officials and land managers.

In addition to field mapping, geologists collect rock samples for laboratory studies, such as chemical and mineralogic analyses, isotopic age determinations, and other physical measurements. Lava samples from active flows are also regularly collected and analyzed to characterize their composition and temperature and how they change over time, which can help reveal the source of the flows.

Samples of spatter erupted from a fissure on Kīlauea's East Rift Zone being collected by an HVO geologist (lower right) in March 2011 (USGS photograph by Matthew R. Patrick).

Gordon A. Macdonald, who came to HVO in 1948 and served as Director from 1951 to 1956, initiated the regular collection of lava samples and was the first HVO scientist to conduct comprehensive studies of the geochemistry and petrology (mineral composition, texture, and origin) of Hawaiian lavas. Subsequent and ongoing petrologic studies have yielded many new insights into the evolution of Hawaiian volcanoes and how they work.

Geologic observations are just as essential today as they were in Jaggar's day to monitoring and understanding volcanic activity in Hawai'i. Early in HVO's history, photographs and movies were the primary means of documenting Kīlauea's and Mauna Loa's eruptive activity. HVO scientists can now capture and view webcam and occasional satellite images of remote eruptive activity without leaving the observatory. These images complement onsite field work, which is still the most direct and preferred method of observation and documentation.

HVO geologist on the rim of Halema'uma'u Crater setting up monitoring instruments, including a webcam to capture images of the active lava lake deep within Kīlauea's summit vent, which formed in 2008 (USGS photograph by Matthew R. Patrick).

Recording and Communicating Monitoring Results

Perhaps the most important part of HVO's monitoring efforts is, as Thomas Jaggar stated, "to keep and publish careful records" of scientists' observations of Hawaiian volcanoes and to "invite the whole world to cooperate." Monitoring and other scientific data—no matter how precise, abundant, and timely—are of little practical use unless the results are communicated effectively to the scientific community, government officials, emergency managers, news media, and the general public.

As it was 100 years ago, keeping fellow scientists and the public informed about Hawai'i's active volcanoes remains one of HVO's top priorities. This goal is accomplished through professional publications and scientific papers; internal quarterly and annual reports; public talks; features posted on HVO's website, such as daily eruption updates, recent earthquake maps, and frequently asked questions; weekly "Volcano Watch" articles; news releases; and community outreach events.

In May 2010, HVO Scientist-in-Charge, Jim Kauahikaua answers questions from the media during a unique Kīlauea milestone—10,000 days of essentially nonstop eruption (USGS photograph by Janet L . Babb).

During Volcano Awareness Month in 2010, an HVO scientist leads a public field trip to Mauna Ulu, the site of an eruption on Kīlauea's East Rift Zone in 1969–1974 (USGS photograph by Ben Gaddis).

"During the past 100 years, we've seen tremendous advances in the methods, tools, and technology used to study Hawaiian volcanoes and a remarkable increase in our understanding of how volcanoes work. But one of the most important research and monitoring tools used today is the same one used by Thomas A. Jaggar, who founded HVO in 1912, and the Hawaiians before him—observation."

Jim Kauahikaua
HVO Scientist-in-Charge, 2011

From Jaggar's Vision to HVO's Current Mission—Assessing Volcano Hazards and Issuing Timely Warnings

From 1902 to 1910, as Thomas Jaggar traveled to the West Indies, Aleutian Islands, Central America, Sicily, and Japan, he observed first hand the destructive effects of volcanic eruptions and earthquakes. The devastation he saw deeply moved Jaggar and led to his vision of protecting human life and property from natural disasters through sound scientific achievement. He believed this goal could be accomplished by establishing Earth observatories where scientists could conduct continuous and long-term studies of volcanic and seismic processes to learn where, how, and why deadly eruptions and damaging earthquakes occur.

As Jaggar learned more about volcanic and seismic processes, he identified four major hazards that had impacted Hawai'i in past years—explosive eruptions, lava flows, earthquakes, and tsunami. Believing that these hazards would again impact the islands' residents and visitors, he advocated for civil preparedness as the next essential step in protecting life and property.

Today, a key element of HVO's mission is to assess the volcanic and seismic hazards of Hawaiian volcanoes, which affect people's lives, activities, and property both directly and indirectly. These hazards include lava flows, ballistic lava fragments (chunks of lava thrown into the air), volcanic-gas emissions, explosive eruptions, and earthquakes.

These photographs show the town of Saint-Pierre, on the island of Martinique in the West Indies, before and after the devastating 1902 explosive eruption of Mount Pélee, in which 28,000 people perished. Seeing the destruction caused by this eruption and other events motivated Thomas Jaggar's work on volcanoes and earthquakes over the next half century. (Photographs by Alfred Lacroix.)

HVO's current mission is guided by the Disaster Relief Act of 1974, which stipulates that ". . . appropriate Federal agencies . . . insure that timely and effective disaster warning is provided." Specifically, in the State of Hawaii, the responsibilities of this Congressional mandate are fulfilled by HVO scientists, who closely monitor Hawaiian volcanoes and earthquakes and keep emergency managers and the public informed through daily (or more frequent) eruption updates posted online, media releases, and other information statements.

In 2007, the USGS developed a Volcanic Activity Alert-Notification System to uniformly convey the relative level of danger posed by volcanoes in the United States. HVO uses this four-tiered system to communicate the state of unrest for Hawai'i's active volcanoes (see box at right).

In keeping with Jaggar's vision and Federal law and policy, HVO continually strives to better understand the mechanisms that produce volcano hazards, find ways to mitigate the negative effects of these hazards, and develop products to effectively communicate scientific findings to the public. Well-informed citizens can help create resilient and relatively safe communities in volcanically active regions.

Volcano Alert Levels Used by USGS Volcano Observatories

Alert Levels are intended to inform people on the ground about a volcano's status and are issued in conjunction with the Aviation Color Code. Notifications are issued for both increasing and decreasing volcanic activity and are accompanied by text with details (as known) about the nature of the unrest or eruption and about potential or current hazards and likely outcomes.

Term	Description
NORMAL	Volcano is in typical background, noneruptive state or, *after a change from a higher level,* volcanic activity has ceased and volcano has returned to noneruptive background state.
ADVISORY	Volcano is exhibiting signs of elevated unrest above known background level or, *after a change from a higher level,* volcanic activity has decreased significantly but continues to be closely monitored for possible renewed increase.
WATCH	Volcano is exhibiting heightened or escalating unrest with increased potential of eruption, timeframe uncertain, **OR** eruption is underway but poses limited hazards.
WARNING	Hazardous eruption is imminent, underway, or suspected.

On the Island of Hawai'i, lava flows are the volcano hazard of greatest concern to most people. This photo taken in November 2010 shows lava flows slowly burying the access road to the Kalapana Gardens subdivision on the south flank of Kilauea Volcano. Nearby homes were threatened by the flows, and the structure shown in the background of the photograph was destroyed by the lava the next day. HVO scientists also have created a lava-flow hazard-zone map of the Island of Hawai'i (see next page), dividing the island into nine zones. This map can be viewed on the HVO website at http://hvo.wr.usgs.gov/hazards/lavazones/. (USGS photograph by Matthew R. Patrick.)

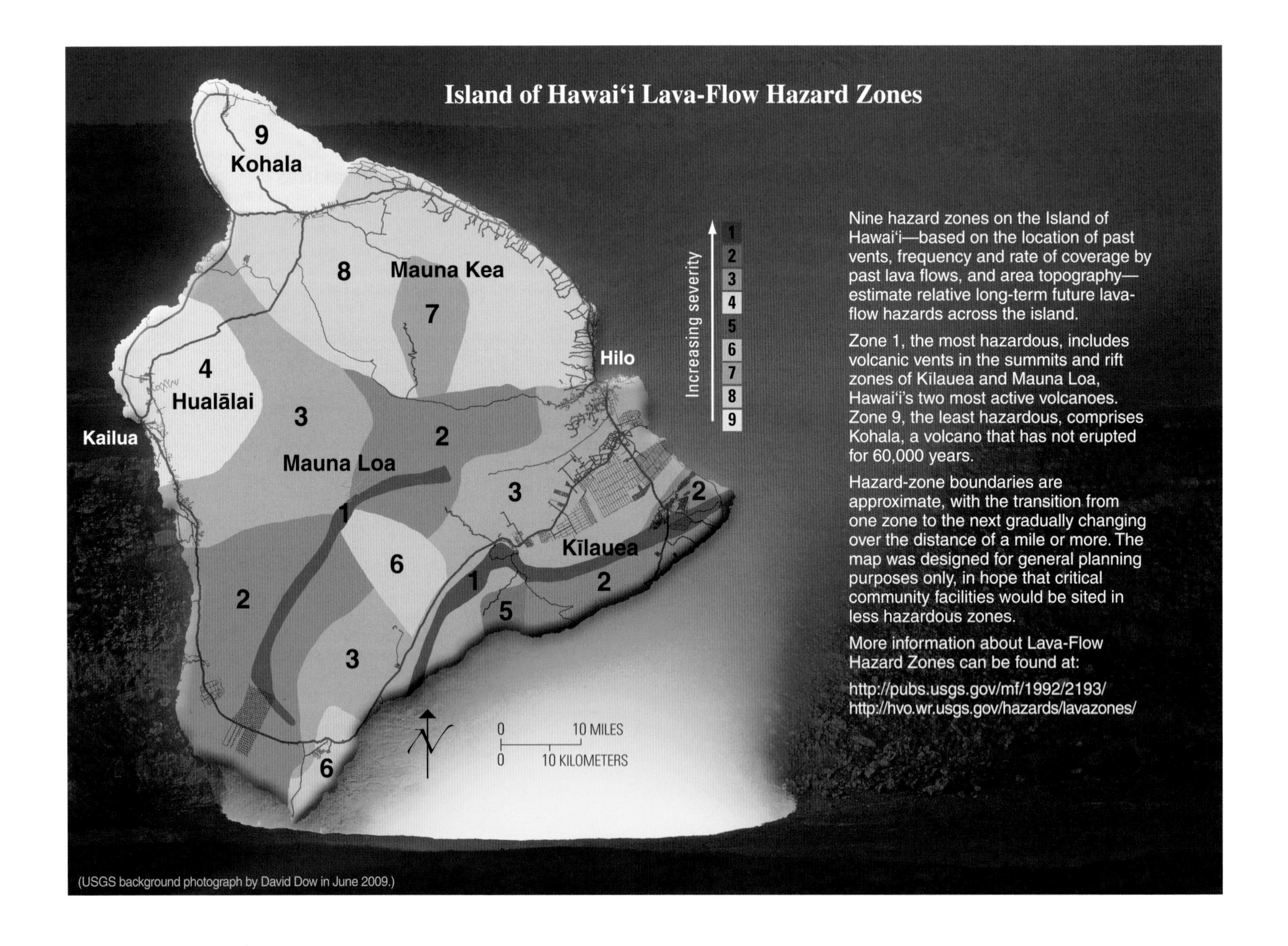

(USGS background photograph by David Dow in June 2009.)

From 1912 to 2012—Discovering How Hawaiian Volcanoes Work

Research conducted by HVO scientists during HVO's first 100 years has resulted in many advances in our understanding of Hawaiian volcanoes and earthquakes. Selected highlights from this century of scientific investigations are discussed below.

Connecting Earthquakes, Volcanic Tremor, and Eruptions

One of Thomas Jaggar's early accomplishments was to confirm that earthquakes and volcanic tremor were closely associated with volcanic activity. The first USGS seismic network installed on the Island of Hawai'i in the 1950s allowed HVO scientists to determine accurate subsurface locations and magnitudes of earthquakes. The locations were sufficiently detailed to provide a method for indirectly observing the movement of magma within a volcano. More sensitive seismic sensors developed and installed in the 1990s now allow HVO scientists to characterize different types of tremor beneath Hawaiian volcanoes, providing even greater detail on the shallow movement and eruption of magma.

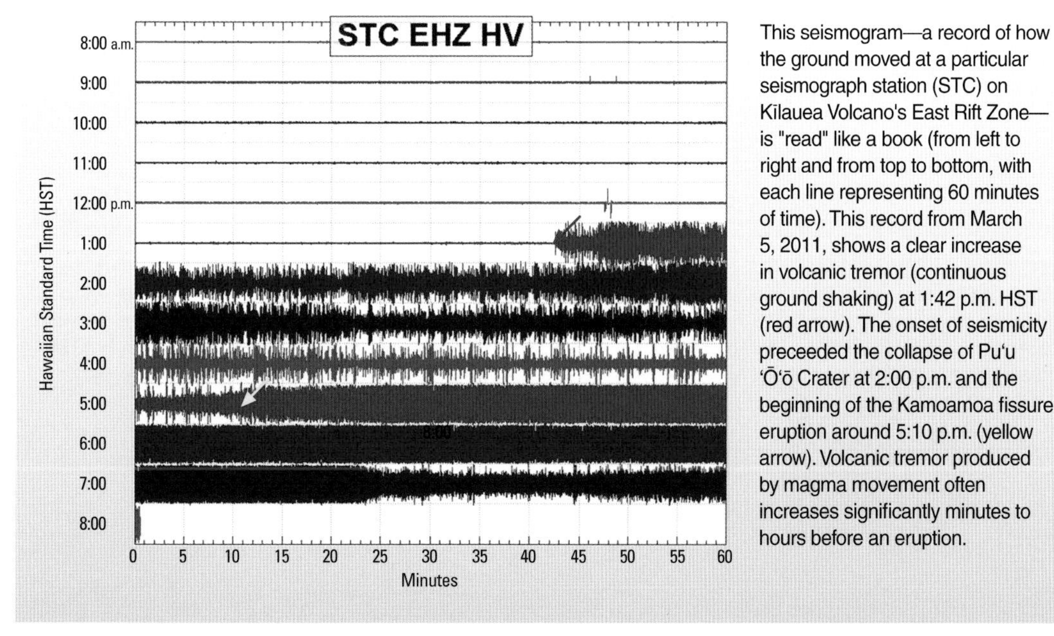

This seismogram—a record of how the ground moved at a particular seismograph station (STC) on Kīlauea Volcano's East Rift Zone—is "read" like a book (from left to right and from top to bottom, with each line representing 60 minutes of time). This record from March 5, 2011, shows a clear increase in volcanic tremor (continuous ground shaking) at 1:42 p.m. HST (red arrow). The onset of seismicity preceeded the collapse of Pu'u 'Ō'ō Crater at 2:00 p.m. and the beginning of the Kamoamoa fissure eruption around 5:10 p.m. (yellow arrow). Volcanic tremor produced by magma movement often increases significantly minutes to hours before an eruption.

Volcanic Gases—Driving Force for Hawaiian Eruptions

Another early scientific accomplishment was discovering that gases dissolved in magma are the main force that drives volcanic eruptions. Volcanic gases account for a tiny fraction—less than one-half of one percent by weight—of magma, which is mostly molten rock. But that small quantity of gas can exert enough force to propel lava fountains many hundreds of feet into the air. Studies of gas compositions and emission rates continue to be an important part of HVO's volcano monitoring and research program.

A lava fountain gushing from the Kīlauea Iki vent on November 18, 1959, as viewed from HVO, about 2 miles away. An early discovery at HVO was that volcanic eruptions, including lava fountains, are mainly driven by expanding volcanic gases. For scale, the wall of Kīlauea Caldera just below the lava fountain is about 130 feet high. (USGS photograph by Jerry Eaton.)

Forecasting Volcanic Eruptions (and Tsunami)

Thomas Jaggar recognized that earthquakes and volcanic tremor provide precursory information that could be used to forecast imminent eruptions. He also found strong evidence that changes in ground deformation (tilt) reflect increasing or decreasing pressure in underground magma bodies and could be used to detect impending volcanic activity.

In the 1950s and 1960s, the development and installation of new and more sensitive monitoring instruments improved HVO's ability to accurately track earthquake migration and the pressurization of subsurface magma reservoirs. Today, in addition to tracking seismicity and deformation, HVO scientists use other monitoring tools and techniques, including measuring volcanic-gas-emission rates, to identify precursory signals of an eruption.

Thomas Jaggar, together with Ruy Finch, also made the connection between earthquakes and tsunami. Using only the few seismometers then available, and noting that seismic waves travel much faster than water waves, they realized that detecting large distant earthquakes could provide hours of warning before the arrival of damaging tsunami in Hawai'i.

After some experimentation, Jaggar issued the first actual tsunami forecast on November 11, 1922, in response to a magnitude 8.5 earthquake that had struck Chile and was recorded on HVO seismometers. Because of this warning, when the tsunami—with waves as high as 10 feet—reached Hawai'i, no lives were lost. Jaggar's and Finch's realization decades ago is still the fundamental basis for current methods used worldwide to forecast tsunami.

Seaward view across the Ku'uali'i Fishpond near Waikoloa on the northwest coast of the Island of Hawai'i. Before the March 11, 2011, tsunami generated by the Tohoku (Japan) magnitude 9.0 earthquake, the fishpond had a wide sand berm and a stone wall between it and the ocean. Tsunami waves overtopped the berm and ultimately destroyed the wall. Because of accurate forecasting and warnings of the 2011 tsunami, there were no injuries in the State of Hawaii. HVO's Thomas Jaggar issued the world's first tsunami forecast on November 11, 1922. (USGS photograph by Andrew Hara.)

Evolution of Hawaiian Volcanoes

In 1946, USGS scientist Harold Stearns was the first to define the evolutionary stages of Hawaiian volcanoes, establishing a basic framework for the geologic history of the Hawaiian Islands. Since then, the availability of abundant and varied data, including data from offshore marine studies, has refined his evolutionary scheme.

Today, scientists generally recognize that Hawaiian volcanoes evolve through several stages. These include a youthful stage in which frequent and voluminous eruptions of fluid lava build a broad "shield" on the ocean floor (Kīlauea and Mauna Loa); a mature post-shield or capping stage characterized by less frequent eruptions of less fluid lava (Hualālai, Mauna Kea, and Haleakalā); and eventually old age, during which erosion rather than eruption is the dominant geologic process (the older Hawaiian volcanoes and islands northwest of east Maui).

The evolutionary stages of Hawaiian volcanoes fit the model of the Pacific tectonic plate (one of about a dozen large plates that make up the rigid outer layer of the Earth) moving across a stationary or slowly migrating "hot spot"—a source of high heat rising from deep within the Earth's interior (mantle) toward the surface. As the Pacific Plate moves slowly to the northwest over the hot spot, the rising heat melts mantle rock, which provides the magma that successively builds the volcanoes of the Hawaiian island chain.

The volcanoes most active now (Kīlauea and Mauna Loa) are thought to be over the center of the hot spot. Hawaiian volcanoes to the northwest are being carried away from the hot spot and into their post-shield phases. In the 1980s, studies of Lō'ihi, the submarine volcano off the southeast coast of the Island of Hawai'i, provided new information on the development of Hawaiian volcanoes by revealing the earliest stage of their evolution.

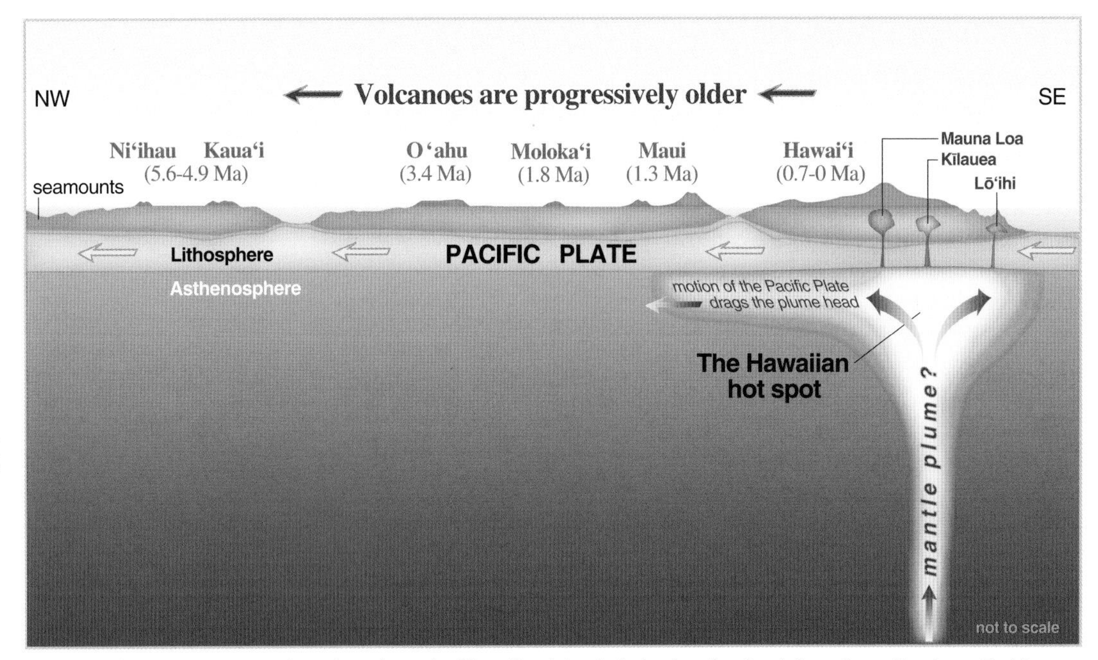

A highly simplified cross-section view along the Hawaiian Island chain showing the inferred mantle plume that has fed the Hawaiian "hot spot" on the overriding Pacific tectonic plate. The geologic ages of the oldest volcano on each island (Ma = millions of years ago) are progressively older to the northwest, consistent with the hot-spot model for the origin of the island chain. (Modified from "This Dynamic Planet," see online resources.)

In the 1980s, imaging the seafloor using side-scan sonar towed from ships, as well as dredging to collect samples of seafloor rocks, provided a detailed picture of the submarine flanks of Hawaiian volcanoes. These surveys confirmed that each of the volcanoes has undergone at least one major flank failure that produced large fields of landslide debris on the ocean floor (see map on inside back cover). The most recent such failure was off the southwest flank of Mauna Loa about 100,000 years ago.

> *"Studying Kīlauea to find out about the beginnings of volcanic evolution is like trying to study early childhood with subjects 40 years old."*
>
> **The late Reggie Okamura**
> **HVO Chief of Operations, 1978–1992**

Internal Structure of Hawaiian Volcanoes

During the late 1960s and 1970s, data from improved seismic instruments allowed scientists to "see" inside Hawaiian volcanoes for the first time using a technique called seismic tomography. As seismic waves pass through subsurface structures, the velocity of the waves changes, allowing the structures and magma pathways within a volcano to be modeled in three dimensions (3D). Current research seeks to include other types of data into the 3D modeling to refine the view and achieve a high-definition, x-ray-like image of Hawaiian volcanoes.

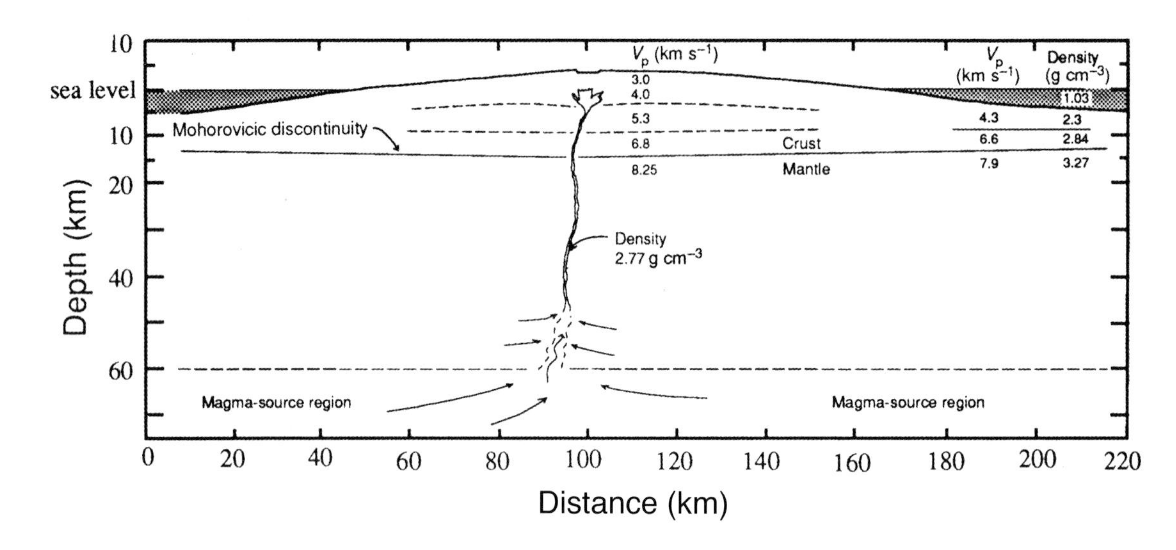

In 1960, Jerry Eaton and Jack Murata proposed a model, based on HVO monitoring data, to show the generalized pathway for magma movement within Kīlauea Volcano from the source region to eruption sites (slightly modified here to remove vertical exaggeration from their original published figure). In this figure, vertical and horizontal distances are shown in "km" (abbreviation for "kilometer," which is equal to 0.62 mile). Although simple and idealized, this "classic" model was revolutionary for its time—and it remains the basic framework for recent refined models reflecting the much more abundant, and higher quality, data acquired since 1960.

Aerial view of Kilauea (foreground), Mauna Loa (left), and Mauna Kea (right) taken in 1983. The smooth low slopes of Mauna Loa indicate the youthful "shield-building" stage of Hawaiian volcano evolution. The steeper slopes and abundant cinder cones on Mauna Kea show that it is in the mature post-shield stage. (USGS photograph by J.D. Griggs.)

"Plumbing Systems" Within Hawaiian Volcanoes

The first viable geophysical model of Hawaiian volcanoes was proposed in 1960. In this model, magma rising from the Earth's mantle is stored in one or more reservoirs beneath a volcano's summit. From these temporary storage areas magma rises to the surface to feed summit eruptions or moves laterally through underground conduits to feed rift-zone (flank) eruptions.

More recently, HVO scientists have tracked migrating sources of inflation before an eruption. This suggests that the main magma reservoir within a volcano occupies a network of interconnected fractures and spaces, with different parts becoming pressurized at different times. Recent seismic studies show shallow structures beneath Kīlauea Caldera, possibly dikes (steeply inclined "blades" of magma), which help explain the location of the summit vent that became active in Halema'uma'u Crater in 2008.

The nature of the conduits that transport magma from the summit to the rift zone is less well known. Recent data have shown that the rift conduit beneath Kīlauea sometimes behaves like a pipe (or pipes), rather than a blade-like dike.

Thomas Jaggar thought that Hawaiian volcanoes shared many common elements. However, as HVO scientists learned more about Kīlauea and Mauna Loa, it became clear that major differences exist between the two volcanoes. For example, Kīlauea erupts more often than Mauna Loa, but over time, Kīlauea erupts smaller volumes of lava. Although the chemistry of their lavas is similar overall, each has a distinct chemical and isotopic signature, so it is possible to distinguish between Kīlauea and Mauna Loa lavas. Scientists now know that no two Hawaiian volcanoes are exactly alike, so each must be studied separately to determine individual characteristics and style of activity.

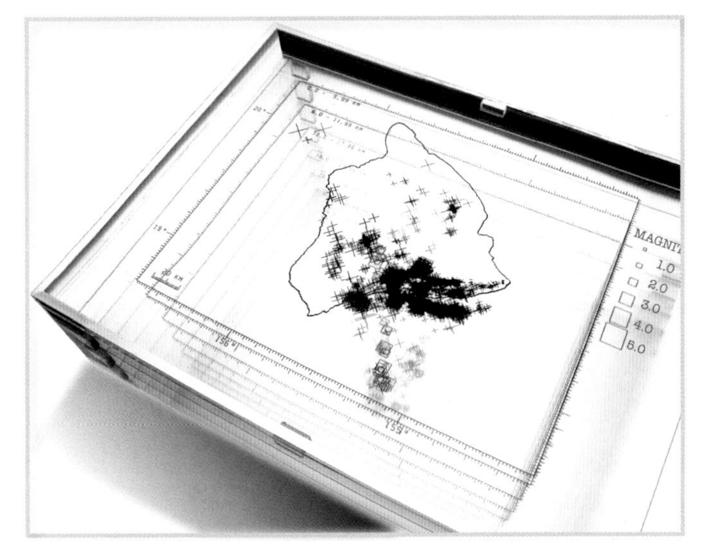

This model shows the three-dimensional (3D) distribution of earthquakes beneath Kīlauea Volcano. Before 3D computer graphics, stacks of plastic layers with maps of earthquakes at sequential depths were used to illustrate subsurface concentrations of seismic activity. This example, built in the 1970s, shows a "plumbing system" within Kīlauea, including lateral conduits feeding the Mauna Ulu East Rift Zone eruption, that is more complex than the Eaton-Murata model. (USGS photograph by James P. Kauahikaua.)

Lava erupting from the Kamoamoa fissure on Kīlauea's East Rift Zone on March 6, 2011, poured into a nearby preexisting ground crack. Deep cracks can form over underground conduits that transport magma from the main reservoir beneath Kīlauea's summit to the East Rift Zone. (USGS photograph by Tim R. Orr.)

Seaward Sliding of Kīlauea's South Flank

In the late 1960s and 1970s, measurements made by HVO scientists revealed that the south flank of Kīlauea Volcano is slowly and steadily sliding toward the sea at a rate of more than 2 inches per year. They also discovered that Kīlauea's south flank is capable of sudden slip that can cause large damaging earthquakes and generate local tsunami like those that occurred in 1868 and 1975. Scientists continue to debate whether magma injected into the East Rift Zone forces the south flank movement or whether the south flank movement creates a space that is then filled by magma.

Another important discovery was that of "slow earthquakes," which were originally identified along subduction zones (zones where two tectonic plates converge and one slides beneath the other) in the late 1990s. But in November 2000, HVO scientists recognized a slow-earthquake-type movement on Kīlauea, during which the volcano's south flank moved more than 2 inches in 36 hours. If such movement had happened over a period of seconds, it would likely have produced a magnitude 5 earthquake. However, because the movement occurred over more than a day, it did not generate perceptible ground shaking. HVO scientists now believe that these slow earthquakes, which can only be detected by sensitive GPS receivers, happen every few years and that their occurrence may explain why large earthquakes do not occur more frequently beneath the south flank.

Aerial view taken in 1987 showing faulting of the south flank of Kīlauea Volcano. In the late 1960s and 1970s, HVO scientists discovered that the south flank of the volcano is slowly and steadily sliding toward the sea at a rate of more than 2 inches per year. This movement to the south from the core of the volcano results in conspicuous ground displacements along faults breaking the surface, as expressed by the cliffs ("pali" in Hawaiian) seen here. (USGS photograph by J.D. Griggs.)

Explosive Eruptions of Hawaiian Volcanoes and Formation of Summit Calderas

Comprehensive geologic mapping of Kīlauea over the past 20 years suggests that the volcano's eruptive activity has alternated between the summit area and locations along the rift zones. Now that HVO has detailed information on the ages of explosive and effusive deposits (such as volcanic ash and lava flows, respectively) at Kīlauea's summit, it is clear that the volcano experiences repetitive cycles of effusive shield building, deep collapse, and explosive eruptions at the summit, followed by renewed shield building. Each such cycle can last for several centuries.

In 1790, just after the arrival of Europeans, columns of volcanic gas and ash rising up to 30,000 feet above Kīlauea were observed during the volcano's most recent explosive eruption cycle. Although the smaller explosive event in 1924 was almost certainly driven by groundwater entering the magma conduit and flashing into steam, the mechanism driving the 1790 explosive eruptions may have been completely different.

Recent investigations of the explosive deposits around Kīlauea's summit indicate that some may have been emplaced by pyroclastic surges (high-speed flows of hot ash and gas that sweep down the flanks of a volcano in an explosive eruption). This sheds new light on Kīlauea's past behavior because pyroclastic surges are normally associated with volcanoes that are thought to be much more explosive than Kīlauea, such as Mount St. Helens, Washington.

Incandescent tephra (volcanic ash and lava fragments) blasted from the Halema'uma'u Crater vent at Kīlauea's summit during an explosive eruption on October 12, 2008. HVO scientists have discovered that, despite Kīlauea's reputation for generally quiet eruptions of lava flows, the volcano has experienced both small and large explosive eruptions in the past, including one in 1790 that killed more than 80 Hawaiians. (USGS still-frame image captured from an HVO time-lapse video.)

Drilling into Lava Lakes—Documenting How Bodies of Molten Rock Cool and Solidify

In late 1959, an eruption at the summit of Kīlauea formed a lava lake 440 feet deep in Kīlauea Iki Crater. Only 4 months after the eruption ended, HVO scientists drilled through the crust of the lava lake (only 9 feet thick at the time) in an experiment to measure temperature and to collect lava and gas samples from the lake. The Kīlauea Iki lava lake was drilled six more times through the years to monitor its cooling history. In 1988, the last time scientists drilled into the lake, only traces of molten rock remained deep inside. Although still hot at depth, the lava lake is believed to have completely solidified by the mid-1990s.

Drilling studies were also carried out on Kīlauea's East Rift Zone in lava lakes at 'Alae and Makaopuhi Craters in 1962 and 1965, respectively. Collectively, the drilling projects on Kīlauea Volcano represented the world's first-ever systematic studies of the cooling, crystallization, and solidification of bodies of molten rock at an active volcano.

In 1990, as pāhoehoe (smooth, billowy, or ropey) lavas from Kīlauea entered the coastal town of Kalapana, several experiments were set up to study the initial stages of lava cooling from the first hours of emplacement to weeks or months later. Data from these lava-flow experiments filled a gap in the lava-lake cooling studies by confirming that lava, whether in a lake or a flow, cools and solidifies at progressively slower rates over time.

Kīlauea Iki Crater was partially filled with lava during an eruption in late 1959, forming a 440-foot-deep lava lake. This view from the rim of the crater shows the drilling operation (circled) on the solid surface of the lava lake in 1975 (USGS photograph by Jerry P. Eaton). A helicopter (inset) was used to lower drilling equipment onto the still steaming crust of the lava lake (USGS photograph by Donald Peterson).

Behavior of Active Lava Lakes

Lava lakes and perched (elevated) ponds of lava produced by Kīlauea's ongoing eruption provide continuing opportunities to observe the dynamics of active lava lakes, first studied by Frank Perret and Thomas Jaggar during the time of HVO's founding. Many questions still exist about how lava lakes can release gas and heat and continue to circulate without cooling and becoming solid.

When first studied, continuous observation of lava lakes was accomplished by observers who took notes and measurements day and night, 7 days a week. Today, time-lapse cameras, video, and webcams are used. Results from these new observation tools have provided a deeper understanding of the mechanics of lava lakes as closed systems. Fresh lava enters the lake as foam or froth, gas is released, and the dense degassed molten lava then circulates back into conduits from which it erupted.

After the floor of Pu'u 'Ō'ō Crater on Kīlauea's East Rift Zone collapsed on March 3, 2011, lava began to refill the crater. In the process, a perched (elevated) lava pond was built, in which lava circulated in an east-west pattern. Perched lava ponds were common within Halema'uma'u Crater at Kīlauea's summit in HVO's early years, as well as during a nearly 1-year-long summit eruption in 1967–1968. (USGS photograph by Tim R. Orr.)

Dynamics of Flowing Lava

Frank Perret's successful measurement in 1911 of the temperature of molten lava—the first in the world—was an early step toward understanding the dynamics of flowing lava. His measurement of 1,850 degrees Fahrenheit is similar to Hawaiian lava temperatures obtained by modern instruments (2,100 degrees Fahrenheit).

Knowledge of how lava flows are supplied and emplaced advanced significantly during recent long-lived Kīlauea eruptions—Mauna Ulu, from 1969 to 1974, and Pu'u 'Ō'ō, the ongoing eruption that began in 1983. Through close and continuous observation of lava-flow dynamics during these eruptions, we now have a greater understanding of pāhoehoe and 'a'ā (rough, blocky) lava-flow textures and the transitions between them. Insights on Hawaiian lava flows have even aided studies of volcanoes on Mars, Venus, and elsewhere in our solar system.

Understanding the role of lava tubes in supplying distant fronts of lava flows has also advanced in the past four decades. Because lava tubes are highly efficient thermal insulators, lava inside them remains hotter and more fluid, which allows the lava to travel much farther from an erupting vent than would be otherwise possible. This provides a viable explanation for the formation of the characteristic broad and gentle slopes of Hawaiian shield volcanoes.

With the aid of digital mapping software and computerized representations of terrain and topography developed in the 1990s, HVO scientists can now accurately forecast likely flow paths and rates of advance for lava flows. These forecasts, which are used to issue advisories to public safety officials, are an important tool to mitigate the risks from volcanic hazards.

The solid roofs of lava tubes sometimes collapse, forming "skylights" that reveal the molten lava flowing inside the tubes. This 2009 oblique aerial view shows a skylight on a tube transporting lava from the source vent at Pu'u 'Ō'ō Crater on Kīlauea's East Rift Zone to a distant ocean entry site (marked by the prominent gas plume), a distance of more than 7 miles. (USGS photograph by James P. Kauahikaua.)

HVO—The next 100 years

As the achievements of the Hawaiian Volcano Observatory's first 100 years are celebrated, the work started by Thomas A. Jaggar in 1912—the careful and systematic study of volcanic and seismic activity—continues. For all that has been learned, many questions about Hawaiian volcanoes remain unanswered, such as: How does the internal "plumbing" of Kīlauea differ from other volcanoes? Can large earthquakes influence future eruptions? Where and why do explosive eruptions on Hawaiian volcanoes occur? These are but a few of the questions that will keep the next generation of HVO scientists busy.

Thomas Jaggar was a generalist in that he used a variety of different types of data to learn how Hawaiian volcanoes work. Since then, scientific researchers have become increasingly more focused, with specialists seeking to extract detailed information from each data type. HVO's future will include developing modern generalist methods to jointly interpret data from seismic, deformation, volcanic-gas, and geologic studies. Doing so will yield volcano models that provide an integrated understanding of volcanic structures and processes.

HVO currently monitors Hawaiian volcanoes and earthquakes with state-of-the-art instruments, thanks in part to the American Recovery and Reinvestment Act of 2009, which funded upgrades and expansion of HVO's monitoring network and telemetry. As 21st century technology advances, new ways of studying volcanic and seismic activity will doubtless be discovered. Whatever the future brings, HVO will continue to be at the forefront in developing, testing, and implementing cutting-edge volcano and seismic monitoring tools and techniques.

Today's scientists are the pioneers of HVO's next 100 years. As these scientists build on previous work and face future opportunities and challenges, Jaggar's vision to "protect life and property on the basis of sound scientific achievement" remains valid and will continue to guide the Hawaiian Volcano Observatory.

Today's scientists are the pioneers of HVO's next 100 years. Here, HVO scientist Kevan Kamibayashi talks about his work on Hawaiian volcanoes with children at the Hilo Public Library in June 2011, hoping to inspire them to become tomorrow's scientists. As a child, Kevan attended a summer geology program on Kīlauea Volcano in 1995 (inset; Kevan at center), at which Jim Kauahikaua, now HVO's Scientist-in-Charge, was a coinstructor. His experience with Jim inspired Kevan to become a scientist, affirming the belief of HVO's founder, Thomas Jaggar, in the value of outreach and education. (Photograph by Moses Gonsalves, Hilo Public Library; inset, USGS photograph by James P. Kauahikaua.)

Online Resources

USGS Hawaiian Volcano Observatory Website
http://hvo.wr.usgs.gov/

USGS Volcano Hazards Program
http://volcanoes.usgs.gov/

USGS Earthquake Hazards Program
http://earthquake.usgs.gov/

USGS Geologic Map of the Island of Hawai'i
http://pubs.usgs.gov/ds/2005/144/

USGS Map Showing Lava-Flow Hazard Zones, Island of Hawai'i
http://pubs.usgs.gov/mf/1992/2193/

"Eruptions of Hawaiian Volcanoes: Past, Present, and Future"
http://pubs.usgs.gov/gip/117/

"Hawaii's Volcanoes Revealed"
http://geopubs.wr.usgs.gov/i-map/i2809/

"Selected Time-Lapse Movies of the East Rift Zone Eruption of Kīlauea Volcano, 2004–2008"
http://pubs.usgs.gov/ds/621/

"This Dynamic Earth: The Story of Plate Tectonics"
http://pubs.usgs.gov/gip/dynamic/

USGS Fact Sheets

"Kīlauea—An Explosive Volcano in Hawai'i"
http://pubs.usgs.gov/fs/2011/3064/

"Earthquakes in Hawai'i—An Underappreciated but Serious Hazard"
http://pubs.usgs.gov/fs/2011/3013/

"Living on Active Volcanoes—The Island of Hawai'i"
http://pubs.usgs.gov/fs/fs074-97/

"Volcanic Air Pollution—A Hazard in Hawai'i"
http://pubs.usgs.gov/fs/fs169-97/

"The Ongoing Pu'u 'Ō'ō—Kupaianaha Eruption of Kīlauea Volcano, Hawai'i"
http://pubs.usgs.gov/fs/2004/3085/

"Monitoring Ground Deformation from Space"
http://pubs.usgs.gov/fs/2005/3025/

Low clouds reflect the glow of molten lava filling the crater atop the Pu‘u ‘Ō‘ō‘ cone on Kīlauea's East Rift Zone on August 2, 2011 (photograph by Scott K. Rowland, University of Hawai‘i at Mānoa).

The Hawaiian Islands, shown in shades of gray with highest areas appearing white, are the tops of massive volcanoes, the bulks of which lie below sea level. Historical lava flows that have erupted from Mauna Loa, Kilauea, and Hualālai volcanoes on the Island of Hawai'i are shown in red. Ocean depths, indicated by colors ranging from orange (shallowest) to green to violet (deepest), are greatest northeast of Maui, where the ocean is 18,865 feet deep. This shaded-relief map shows the seafloor surrounding the Hawaiian Islands as if the Pacific Ocean had been drained away. Hummocky landslide deposits—from gradual slumping or sudden collapse of volcano flanks in the geologic past—are visible north of O'ahu and Moloka'i and immediately west of the Island of Hawai'i. The map (reduced for this publication) is from "Hawaii's Volcanoes Revealed" (see list of online resources).

Produced in the Menlo Park Publishing Service Center
Manuscript approved for publication, November 7, 2011
Edited by James W. Hendley II and Peter H. Stauffer
Layout and design by Jeanne S. DiLeo